Two Sides to Every Discussion 2

英語で考え、英語で発信する 2

Jonathan Lynch

Kotaro Shitori

SEIBIDO

音声ファイルのダウンロード／ストリーミング

CD マーク表示がある箇所は、音声を弊社 HP より無料でダウンロード／ストリーミングすることができます。トップページのバナーをクリックし、書籍検索してください。書籍詳細ページに音声ダウンロードアイコンがございますのでそちらから自習用音声としてご活用ください。

https://www.seibido.co.jp

Two Sides to Every Discussion 2

はじめに

　近年の英語教育では、従来の文法を重視した「読むこと」「書くこと」に代わり、「聞くこと」「話すこと」を主体とするコミュニケーションの重要性が声高に叫ばれています。これが果たしてどのような結果をもたらすことになるのか、確かなことは現時点では推測の域を出ません。ですが、ただひとつ明らかなことがあります。それは、よく言われていることですが、英語は世界の人々と意思疎通を図るための単なるツールにすぎないということです。

　海外で生活すると切実に感じることでもありますが、他者に向けて自分の意見を表明することは、自分がどんな人間なのかを相手に深く理解してもらうための最も有効な手段であると同時に、自分の存在を認めてもらうために避けて通れないものでもあります。確かに、協調性が過度に重んじられる日本では、自分の意見を持つこと、そしてそれを主張することは、必ずしも周囲から好意的に受け入れられるとは限りません。それは多くの帰国子女の皆さんが実際に経験していることでもあります。ですが、こうした状況は世界的に見ても極めてまれであると言わざるを得ません。

　そうした意味でも、大切なのは近年の英語教育が目指している「英語が話せるようになること」ではなく、まずはその大前提として、「自分の意見をしっかり持つこと」なのです。ですから、「英語が話せるようになること」を一番の目標に設定する前に、まずは自分の内面とじっくり向き合って、人とは違うあなたらしい考えを持つことに意識の目を向けてください。それができるようになってから、英語というツールを使って発信できるように本格的に努力し始めても遅すぎることはありません。あなたが何者なのかを知ろうとする相手を前にして大事なことは、どう話すかではなく、何を話すかなのです。

　本テキストは、好評だった前作の「Two Sides to Every Discussion—英語で考え、英語で発信する」の続編として企画され、内容もすべて一新されています。そして、「若者文化」「社会問題」「旅行」「ライフスタイル」「科学技術」といった実に多岐にわたる分野から、皆さんにとって身近な話題が数多く取り上げられています。これらのテーマを前にしてあなたはどう考えるのか、ほかの人とは異なる独自の視点からひとつでも多くのユニークかつ説得力ある意見が出ることを、著者として楽しみにしています。

　最後になりましたが、本テキストの出版に際し、（株）成美堂編集部の小亀正人氏、佐藤公雄氏には大変御世話になりました。この場を借りて心より御礼申し上げます。

Jonathan Lynch

委文　光太郎

本書の使い方

Pre-Reading Vocabulary Task

本文中で使用されている重要な単語や熟語が選び出されています。それぞれの正しい意味を、A～Hから選んでください。なお、分からない語句でも辞書は使わず、推測して答えてみましょう。

Reading

まずは、辞書を使わずに本文を一通り読んでみましょう。そしてそれが終わったら、今度は辞書を使用して、分からない単語や熟語の意味を調べながら何度もじっくりと読んでみましょう。最後に、音声を聞きながら音読することをお勧めします。

Note

固有名詞や難しい語句の意味が説明されています。必要なときには参考にしてください。

Comprehension

本文の内容が正確に理解されているかを確認するための質問です。該当する段落の番号を空欄に書き入れた上で、for または against のどちらかを○で囲んでください。

Grammar Point

本文中で使用されている重要な文法事項が、簡潔に解説されています。本文を理解するための参考にしてください。

Writing

自分の意見を英語で書けるようになるための練習です。参考になる例文が数多く提示されていますので、難しいと感じたときはそれらを参考にしてください。

Listening Dictation

何の準備もなくいきなり音声を聞いて空欄を埋める方法も可能ですが、英文のおおよその意味を事前に理解した上で音声を聞くことをお勧めします。問題が難しい場合は、先生に頼んで音声を何回も聞かせてもらいましょう。

Speaking

毎回のテーマに基づいた会話モデルが提示されていますので、それを使用してクラスメートや先生にあなたの意見を伝えてみましょう。また、Writing で作成した英文もここで積極的に使用してみてください。

Column

毎回のテーマについてさらに深く理解してもらうために、短いコラムが載せてあります。時間があれば、ぜひ読んでください。

CONTENTS

Unit 1 Shared Housing vs. Living Alone

一人暮らし

シェアハウス

テレビ番組の影響などもあってシェアハウスの人気が上昇しています。選ぶとしたら、あなたはシェアハウスと一人暮らしのどちらがよいですか。

Pre-Reading Vocabulary Task

次の語句の日本語の意味として最も適切なものを、A〜Hから選んで（　　）に記入しましょう。

1. atmosphere	（　）	A.	雰囲気
2. empty	（　）	B.	魅力的な
3. on the other hand	（　）	C.	比較すると
4. in comparison	（　）	D.	これに対して、他方では
5. attractive	（　）	E.	欠如、不足
6. in reality	（　）	F.	残念な、不運な
7. lack	（　）	G.	誰もいない、空っぽの
8. unfortunate	（　）	H.	実際には

一人暮らしよりも
シェアハウスの方がいい

 02

For

[1] Living in a shared house or apartment is becoming more common among young people in Japan. In fact, living in shared accommodations is better than living alone for several reasons.

[2] First, it is easier to make new friends in a shared house. Everybody makes an effort to get along, thus creating a very friendly atmosphere. By sharing household chores and making a pleasant living environment together, strong bonds of friendship will certainly be formed.

[3] Second, if you live alone, returning to an empty home can be depressing, especially after a hard day. A shared house on the other hand, is much livelier. If you feel down, you can talk and vent with housemates in the evening!

[4] Finally, living in a shared house is safer. A person living alone could be vulnerable to a robbery. In comparison, a home invasion, for example, is much less likely in a shared house.

 03

Against

[5] On the face of it, the idea of living in a shared house or apartment might seem attractive. However, in reality, this is not a recommended option. Living alone is preferable for the following reasons.

[6] First and foremost, living alone is easier than living in a shared house. In the latter situation, you might end up sharing accommodations with a disagreeable person or even a strange person. Surely that would be difficult to endure.

[7] Second, in shared accommodations, there is a loss of privacy to some degree. Usually, housemates share the living room, kitchen and bathroom areas. Although your own room is private, the general lack of privacy may be too much.

[8] Finally, it is an unfortunate fact that some people are not particularly clean. They do not clean up after themselves and leave places in a mess. Thus, if you are unlucky with your housemates, shared accommodations might be dirtier or messier than a private apartment.

Note

shared house シェアハウス（数人が共同で生活する住居） **shared accommodations** 共同の宿泊施設 **get along** 仲良く暮らす **household chores** 家事（chores は「雑用」の意味） **living environment** 生活環境 **bonds** 絆 **depressing** 憂鬱な **lively** にぎやかな **feel down** 気分が落ち込む **vent** 発散する **housemate** 同居人 **be vulnerable to ～** ～に対して無防備だ **robbery** 強盗 **home invasion** 押し込み強盗 **on the face of it** 一見したところでは **preferable** 好ましい **first and foremost** 何よりもまず **the latter** 後者の **end up ～ing** 最終的に～になる **disagreeable** 嫌な **to some degree** ある程度 **clean up after ～** ～が汚した場所をきれいにする **in a mess** 散らかして

Comprehension

次の文は本文の内容を要約したものです。該当する段落の番号を空欄に書き入れて、for または against のどちらに書かれているか○で囲んでください。

1 Some people do not have high standards of cleanliness. ☐ for against

2 It might be hard to maintain privacy. ☐ for against

3 There is no need to feel lonely in this type of accommodations. ☐ for against

4 One or more of your housemates might be unpleasant in some way. ☐ for against

5 There is a chance to make many good friends. ☐ for against

6 People are safer in this type of accommodations. ☐ for against

Grammar Point 　形式主語の it

1. 不定詞句が真の主語である場合

*First, **it** is easier **to** make new friends in a shared house.* [第2段落]

2. that節が真の主語である場合

*Finally, **it** is an unfortunate fact **that** some people are not particularly clean.* [第8段落]

*fact that ... は「…という事実」という意味の「同格の that」としてよく使用されるが、ここでは形式主語 it の内容を表す真主語の that として用いられている。

例）The car accident was due to the fact that the driver was careless.

Writing

以下の例文を参考にしながら、比較級の形容詞を使用した表現を学習しましょう。
まずは本文中の For のセクションから次の文を探してください。

1. In fact, living in shared accommodations **is better than** living alone for several reasons.

２つの物事を比べる際に比較級の形容詞を使うと、両者の長所や短所が明確になります。For と Against のセクションには、比較級の形容詞を使った文がほかにもあるので見つけてください。

例文をあと２つ追加します。

2. Living in shared accommodations **is more fun than** living alone. You can have a party with your housemates!
3. Living alone might **be harder** because you have to do everything by yourself.

それでは賛成か反対の立場を決めた上で、肯定的または否定的な意味を持つ形容詞の比較級を使用しながら、該当する空欄を英語で埋めてみましょう。

I think living in a shared house is _____ than living alone.

_____

OR

I think living alone is _____ than living in a shared house.

_____

Listening Dictation

04

音声を聞いて次の空欄を埋めましょう。

1. Many university students in the United States live in shared houses and even if they live in a [1] ( ) they might share a [2] ( ) with another student.

2. If you live in shared accommodations, it is important to have a sense of [1] ( ) and a sense of [2] ( ) for your housemates.

3. At the moment I live with my [1] ( ) but after [2] ( ) I am planning to live alone in an apartment for the first time.

4

Speaking

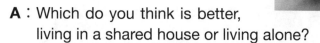

次の会話モデルを使用して、クラス
メートや先生にあなたの意見を伝え
てみましょう。また、先ほど学習した
表現も積極的に使いましょう。

A：Which do you think is better,
living in a shared house or living alone?

B：Now that's an interesting question! Let me see.

To be honest, I think living in a shared house is better.

or

To be honest, I think living alone is better.

A：Why?

B：Well, [reason]_____

A：Sure. Any other reasons?

B：Also, [reason]_____

A：OK! I can understand your point of view.

B：How about you? Which do you think is better?

A：Actually, I think living in a shared house is better (too).

or

Actually, I think living alone is better (too).

B：Why's that?

A：[reason]_____

　シェアハウスは海外では昔から一般的です。例えば英国の大学生の
場合、入学して数年間は大学の寮で暮らすことができますが、高学年
になると寮から出て行くよう求められることがあります。そのような場
合、近隣のフラット（flat）と呼ばれる住宅を借りて、友人や知り合いた
ちとシェアして暮らすことが普通です。大学内の掲示板には、「Room
for Rent（部屋を貸します）」のちらしがよく貼り出されていますが、
貼られたその日に借り手が見つかることも少なくないようです。

Unit 2 Studying in a Café vs. Home

試験前なのに勉強する気が起きない。そんなときにカフェを利用する人は少なくないかもしれません。あなたはカフェと自宅、どちらで勉強することが多いですか。

Pre-Reading Vocabulary Task

次の語句の日本語の意味として最も適切なものを、A〜Hから選んで（　　）に記入しましょう。

1. desired	（　）	**A.**	環境
2. environment	（　）	**B.**	迷惑
3. temperature	（　）	**C.**	〜を広げる
4. affect 〜	（　）	**D.**	望ましい
5. narrow	（　）	**E.**	〜に影響を与える
6. spread out 〜	（　）	**F.**	温度
7. concentrate on 〜	（　）	**G.**	〜に集中する
8. nuisance	（　）	**H.**	狭い

勉強するなら自宅よりもカフェだ

 05

For

[1] To get your desired grades on tests you need to put in long hours of study. But where is the best place to do it? Given the choice between studying at home or studying in a café, which would you choose?

[2] We say that a café is better for the following reasons. 5

[3] For a start, a café has an agreeable atmosphere. People go there to spend a pleasant time. That nice environment can lift our spirits and make studying seem less of a chore.

[4] In addition, a café serves delicious drinks and food. Having a cup of coffee, tea or fruit juice perks us up and allows us to study more 10 effectively. And, of course, we do not have to waste time making it ourselves.

[5] Last but not least, the temperature in a café is always perfect for study. As everybody knows, when studying or working, the temperature affects your productivity. At home, it might be too cold in winter or too 15 hot in summer.

 06

Against

[6] These days we often see high school students and university students studying in cafés. But is that a good choice?

[7] We say no for the following reasons. 20

[8] First, a café may feel cramped. Often cafés are quite crowded and the tables on either side are being used by other people. In addition, the tables are usually narrower than a desk at home—there is no space to spread out our books.

[9] Second, in a word, noise. As everybody knows, there is almost 25 always some noise in cafés. Whether background music, noise from behind the counter, or other customers talking, a café is simply too noisy to concentrate on study.

[10] Finally, we should think about other café users. If we hog a table for hours and hours, people who want to have a quick cup of coffee 30 may not be able to find a seat. To state it plainly, people studying in cafés are a nuisance.

[11] All in all, a quiet desk or table at home is a preferable place to study.

Unit 2

Note

grade 成績　**put in long hours of study** 長時間勉強をする（put in は「（仕事などを）する」の意味）　**Given the choice between A or B** A か B を選ぶことができるなら（Given ～ で「～が与えられると」を意味する）　**for a start** まず第一に〔口語〕　**agreeable** 居心地のよい　**lift one's spirits** ～を元気づける（= perk ～ up）　**less of a chore** それほど苦ではない（a chore は「つらい仕事」の意味）　**waste time doing** …して時間を無駄にする（time の後に in が省略されている）　**last but not least** 大事なことを言い忘れたが（「最後に述べるが重要さはこれまで述べたことに劣らない」というのが本来の意味）　**productivity** 生産性　**cramped** 窮屈な　**on either side** 両側の（= on both sides）　**are being used**（「be 動詞 + being + 過去分詞」は「～されているところだ」を表す受動態の進行形）　**in a word** 一言で言えば　**hog ～** ～を独り占めする　**for hours and hours** 何時間も　**to state it plainly** はっきり言うと　**all in all** 全般的に見て

Comprehension

次の文は本文の内容を要約したものです。該当する段落の番号を空欄に書き入れて、for または against のどちらに書かれているか○で囲んでください。

1 We can get refreshments here which energize us.　☐　for　against

2 It is selfish to use a table for a long time.　☐　for　against

3 A table here is too narrow for effective study.　☐　for　against

4 This location provides a pleasant environment for studying.　☐　for　against

5 It is noisy here so we cannot focus on work.　☐　for　against

6 The temperature here is always suitable for study.　☐　for　against

Grammar Point 　　Whether の用法

**Whether** background music, noise from behind the counter, **or** other customers talking, a café is simply too noisy to concentrate on study.
[第9段落]

* Whether A, B, or C「A であろうと B であろうと C であろうと」を意味する。上の文の場合、Whether の後に it is が省略されている。この他に Whether A or B で「A かまたは B か」を意味することもある。

例）I don't know whether it is true or not.

8

Writing

以下の例文を参考にしながら、「**誰もが知っているように**」という表現を学習しましょう。まずは、本文中の For のセクションから次の文を探してください。

1. **As everybody knows,** when studying or working, the temperature affects your productivity.

<As everybody knows, ... > は、明らかかもしれないがそれでも述べる価値があると判断したときに文頭で使います。なお、この表現は自らの主張の妥当性を強調する働きがありますが、少し傲慢に聞こえてしまう恐れもあるので控えめに使うことをお勧めします。Against のセクションにも同様の表現があるので確認しましょう。

例文をあと2つ紹介します。参考にしてください。

2. **As everybody knows,** caffeine in tea or coffee acts as a stimulant and can help us to keep studying for a long time.
3. **As everybody knows,** we are less likely to waste time at home, especially when our parents are there.

それでは賛成か反対の立場を決めた上で、学習した表現を使用しながら、英語で空欄を埋めてみましょう。

FOR : I think a café is preferable for studying. As everybody knows, ___

_____

OR

AGAINST : I think home is preferable for studying. As everybody knows,

_____

Listening Dictation

07

音声を聞いて次の空欄を埋めましょう。

1. As everybody knows, ¹⁾(   ) for study is more important than ²⁾(   ).

2. I can only study in a café ¹⁾(   ) has a no-smoking ²⁾(   ).

3. I have two younger ¹⁾(   ) so actually my home is ²⁾(   ).

Speaking

次の会話モデルを使用して、クラスメートや先生にあなたの意見を伝えてみましょう。また、先ほど学習した表現も積極的に使いましょう。

A：Which do you prefer, studying in a café or studying at home?

B：Hmm... that's tricky.

I guess I prefer studying in a café.

or

I guess I prefer studying at home.

A：Really? How come?

B：Well, [reason]_____

A：Sure. Any other reasons?

B：Also, [reason]_____

A：I see.

B：How about you? Which do you prefer?

A：Actually, I prefer studying in a café (too).

or

Actually, I prefer studying at home (too).

B：Why's that?

A：[reason]_____

　　カフェで勉強をする人が増えたせいかもしれませんが、最近では勉強や仕事を禁止するカフェが増加しています。書店とカフェがコラボした店舗でさえ、「混雑時の勉強とパソコン作業の禁止、本の持ち込みは1人1冊まで」と書かれた立て看板が入り口付近に設置されていることがあります。

　　すべてのカフェで勉強が禁止にならないようにするためにも、①朝や夕方など比較的空いている時間帯を利用する②混雑してきたらすぐに席を立つ③店員さんに声をかけられたら素直に席を譲る——などを常に心掛ける必要があるかもしれません。

Unit 3 Gakuran vs. Blazer

今やブレザーに主役の座を奪われつつある学ランですが、高校の制服としてあなたはどちらの方が好きですか。またその理由は何ですか。

Pre-Reading Vocabulary Task

次の語の日本語の意味として最も適切なものを、A〜Hから選んで（　　）に記入しましょう。

1. military （　　）　　　**A.** 特徴的な

2. appearance （　　）　　　**B.** 組み合わせ

3. distinctive （　　）　　　**C.** 軍人らしい、軍隊の

4. neat （　　）　　　**D.** 堅い

5. valuable （　　）　　　**E.** 外見

6. advantage （　　）　　　**F.** 価値のある、貴重な

7. stiff （　　）　　　**G.** こざっぱりした、きちんとした

8. combination （　　）　　　**H.** 有利な点

高校の制服といえば
ブレザーよりも学ランだ

☐1 *Gakuran*-style school uniforms are common for schoolboys in Japan. The stand-up collar and somewhat military appearance are certainly distinctive, especially when compared to a blazer and tie.

5 ☐2 In fact, gakuran uniforms are better than blazer-and-tie styles for the following reasons.

☐3 First and foremost, the gakuran style looks very cool. The stand-up collar and the buttons that go all the way down the jacket provide a manly silhouette. Without doubt, boys wearing the gakuran uniform
10 look both neat and strong at the same time.

☐4 In addition, gakuran uniforms have a long history in Japan. They were introduced in the 19th century and are still popular today. The gakuran style has become a Japanese tradition and this makes it special and valuable.

15 ☐5 Finally, the gakuran uniform is simple and easy to wear. There is no tie and it can be put on quickly. For boys getting ready for school in the morning, this is a big advantage.

☐6 Although it might be hard for them to say so, boys want to look good in their school uniforms. They want a style that will
20 make a good memory for the rest of their lives. That style is a blazer and tie for the following reasons.

☐7 Above all, a blazer-and-tie uniform looks fashionable. The shirt, tie and jacket are a perfect set. Furthermore, many attractive variations in color and style are possible, providing unique uniforms for each school.

25 ☐8 Secondly, the blazer-and-tie uniform is very comfortable. The jacket hangs nicely on the shoulders, with a collar that is not high or stiff around the neck. The material is relatively light and feels smooth to touch.

☐9 Finally, after high school and college, many young men will need
30 to wear a business suit at work. A blazer, shirt and tie combination looks similar to a suit and thus boys can get used to dressing for business.

Note

stand-up collar 立ち襟 **somewhat** やや、多少 **cool** かっこいい〔口語〕 **go all the way down ~** ~の上から下までを占める (all the way down は「端から端まで」の意味) **manly** 男性的な **silhouette** シルエット、輪郭 **without doubt** 確かに (doubtless や no doubt よりも強い確信を示す) **look good in ~** ~が似合う **for the rest of one's lives** 今後ずっと **fashionable** おしゃれな **variation** 変化、バリエーション **hang nicely on ~** ~にフィットする (hang on は「かかる」の意味) **material** 素材 **at work** 職場で (work は名詞) **and thus** …なので **get used to ~ing** ~に慣れる (to は前置詞) **dress for ~** ~に適した服装をする

Comprehension

次の文は本文の内容を要約したものです。該当する段落の番号を空欄に書き入れて、for または against のどちらに書かれているか○で囲んでください。

1 This uniform looks stylish and has many variations. ☐ for against

2 This uniform feels pleasant to wear. ☐ for against

3 This uniform has been worn in Japan for a long time. ☐ for against

4 This uniform looks cool. ☐ for against

5 This uniform is easy to put on in the morning. ☐ for against

6 This uniform prepares boys for the business world. ☐ for against

Grammar Point 現在分詞の形容詞用法

1. 名詞の前に現在分詞が置かれる場合
   - *In fact, gakuran uniforms are better than blazer-and-tie styles for the **following** reasons.* [第2段落]
   - *That style is a blazer and tie for the **following** reasons.* [第6段落]
     *現在分詞が単独で用いられる場合は、名詞 (reasons) の前に置く。

2. 名詞の後に現在分詞が置かれる場合
   - *Without doubt, boys **wearing** the gakuran uniform look both neat and strong at the same time.* [第3段落]
   - *For boys **getting** ready for school in the morning, this is a big advantage.* [第5段落]
     *目的語や補語、修飾語句などを伴う場合は、名詞 (boys) の後に置く。

Writing

以下の例文を参考にしながら、「〜に見える」という表現を学習しましょう。
まずは、本文中の For のセクションから次の文を探してください。

    1. First and foremost, the gakuran style **looks** very cool.

<look ＋ 形容詞> は、ある物の外見について肯定的または否定的な意見を述べるときに役立ちます。Against のセクションにも同様の文があるので探してみましょう。

この他にも例文を2つ挙げておきます。

    2. A gakuran-style uniform **looks** traditional.
    3. A blazer-and-tie-style uniform **looks** a little less formal than the gakuran style.

それでは賛成か反対の立場を決めた上で、学習した表現を使用しながら、英語で空欄を埋めてみましょう。

FOR : I think a gakuran-style uniform is best for boys. _____

_____

OR

AGAINST : I think a blazer-and-tie-style uniform is best for boys. _____

_____

Listening Dictation 10

音声を聞いて次の空欄を埋めましょう。

1. The [1] (   ) of junior and senior high schools in the United States do not have uniforms but many have a dress code that students must [2] (   ).

2. The [1] (   ) that students used to wear with the gakuran uniform in the old days is [2] (   ) seen now.

3. A blazer-and-tie-style uniform might be [1] (   ) on warm days but a gakuran-style uniform is probably [2] (   ) on cool days.

Speaking

次の会話モデルを使用して、クラスメートや先生にあなたの意見を伝えてみましょう。また、先ほど学習した表現も積極的に使いましょう。

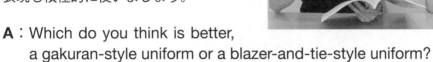

A：Which do you think is better,
a gakuran-style uniform or a blazer-and-tie-style uniform?

B：For me, a gakuran-style uniform is better.

or

For me, a blazer-and-tie-style uniform is better.

A：Is that so? Could you tell me why?

B：Sure. [reason]_____

A：That's interesting. Anything else?

B：Also, [reason]_____

A：I see.

B：How about you? Which style do you think is better?

A：Actually, I think the gakuran style is better (too).

or

Actually, I think the blazer-and-tie-style is better (too).

B：Why's that?

A：[reason]_____

　厳密な調査ではありませんが、大手制服メーカーの担当者によると、現在ではブレザーが約7割を占めていて、学ランは3割にすぎないそうです。

　そして、ブレザーの制服が普及したのは1980年代後半からといわれています。学ランからブレザーに切り替えた理由の1つに、当時流行していた「短ラン（裾の短い学生服）」や「ボンタン（だぼだぼの学生服）」をやめさせる狙いがあったようです。また、修学旅行で海外に行く際に学ランを着ていくと、訪問先の人々に過去の戦争を想起させてしまう、という理由でブレザーに替えた学校もあったようです。

Unit 4 Coming-of-Age Ceremonies

何かとニュースで話題に上ることの多い成人式ですが、皆さんは出席する予定ですか（出席しましたか）。また、日本の成人式についてどう思いますか。

Pre-Reading Vocabulary Task

次の語の日本語の意味として最も適切なものを、A〜Hから選んで（　　）に記入しましょう。

1. passage   (　　)   **A.** 率直な

2. participant   (　　)   **B.** 〜を避ける

3. abolish 〜   (　　)   **C.** 〜を廃止する

4. frank   (　　)   **D.** 参加者

5. contain 〜   (　　)   **E.** 機会

6. opportunity   (　　)   **F.** 重要な

7. avoid 〜   (　　)   **G.** 入口、一節

8. significant   (　　)   **H.** 〜を含む

成人式は廃止するべきだ

For

1 Coming-of-Age Day marks the passage into adulthood for young people in Japan. Although many participants organize private parties for themselves, there are also coming-of-age ceremonies organized by local governments.

2 We propose abolishing coming-of-age ceremonies for the following reasons. 5

3 First, let's be frank... the ceremonies are tedious. They put a damper on what should be a happy day. Young people have suffered similar ceremonies many times already. They do not need another one.

4 Second, unfortunately, the speeches during the ceremonies are predictable. They usually contain advice and encouragement that young adults have heard countless times before. 10

5 Finally, these ceremonies have occasionally become an opportunity for rebellious young adults to cause trouble. Instead of a long-winded ceremony, an enjoyable event is more suitable and could help to avoid such problems. 15

Against

6 Coming-of-Age Day in Japan is a wonderful occasion for young people. More than anything, it is a day of optimism and hope.

7 As the centerpiece of Coming-of-Age Day, we propose that the coming-of-age ceremony should be kept for the following reasons. 20

8 First, the coming-of-age ceremony serves to mark a very important event—the passage into adulthood. Because this is a highly significant occasion, a serious and solemn ceremony is most appropriate.

9 Second, the ceremony provides a focus for Coming-of-Age Day. 25 Without the ceremony, young people would just gather in small groups here and there. As a result, Coming-of-Age Day would lose its importance as a national holiday.

10 Finally, during the coming-of-age ceremony, the mayor of the city and other important people give great life advice to the participants. 30 Drawing on their own experiences, their speeches are full of wonderful guidance and provide inspiration to young adults.

Comprehension

次の文は本文の内容を要約したものです。該当する段落の番号を空欄に書き入れて、for または against のどちらに書かれているか○で囲んでください。

1 The ceremony may be a magnet for troublemakers. ☐ for against

2 The ceremony is a suitable way to celebrate an important occasion. ☐ for against

3 The ceremony itself is boring. ☐ for against

4 The ceremony brings many people together on Coming-of-Age Day. ☐ for against

5 The speeches at the ceremony contain nothing new for the participants. ☐ for against

6 The speechmakers at the ceremony give valuable advice to participants. ☐ for against

Grammar Point   if を使わない仮定法

***Without the ceremony**, young people would just gather in small groups here and there.* ［第9段落］

*Without ～ には「～がなければ / なかったら」という2つの意味がある。動詞が出てこないので、主節の動詞（would gather）からどちらの意味になるのかを判断する。

　　<would + 動詞の原形> ⇒ 仮定法過去 ⇒ ～がなければ
　　<would + have + 過去分詞> ⇒ 仮定法過去完了 ⇒ ～がなかったら

さらに、Without the ceremony は If it were not for the ceremony に書き換えられる。

例) Without the ceremony, young people would have just gathered in small groups here and there.

　　= If it had not been for the ceremony, young people would have just gathered in small groups here and there.

Writing

以下の例文を参考にしながら、「**より [最も] 適している**」という表現を学びましょう。まずは、本文中の For のセクションから次の文を探してください。

1. **Instead of** a long-winded ceremony, an enjoyable event **is more suitable** and could help to avoid such problems.

<Instead of X, Y is more/most suitable.> や <Because ..., Y is more/most suitable.>という表現は、与えられた状況の中で何が適切かを述べる際に使われます（suitable 以外に appropriate も使用可）。Against のセクションにも同様の文があるので探しましょう。

このほかにも例文を 2 つ挙げておきます。

2. **Instead of** winter, a warmer season **is more suitable** for Coming-of-Age Day.
3. **Because** young people have plans to celebrate with friends, a short ceremony **is most appropriate** for Coming-of-Age Day.

それでは賛成か反対の立場を決めた上で、学習した表現を使用しながら、英語で空欄を埋めてみましょう。

FOR : I think coming-of-age ceremonies should be abolished. _____

_____

OR

AGAINST : I think we should keep coming-of-age ceremonies. _____

_____

Listening Dictation

 13

音声を聞いて次の空欄を埋めましょう。

1. I ¹⁾ (   ) my coming-of-age ceremony and the speech by the mayor was interesting because he included some ²⁾ (   ).

2. Instead of a ¹⁾ (   ), I am planning to wear a ²⁾ (   ) at my coming-of-age ceremony.

3. A ceremony was suitable for the older ¹⁾ (   ) but times have changed so a visit to a ²⁾ (   ) ³⁾ (   ) is more appropriate these days, I think.

19

Speaking

次の会話モデルを使用して、クラス
メートや先生にあなたの意見を伝え
てみましょう。また、先ほど学習した
表現も積極的に使いましょう。

A：Do you think that coming-of-
age ceremonies should be abolished?

B：That's a tricky question!

Well, yes, I do.

or

Well, no, I don't.

A：Really? Why's that?

B：[reason]＿＿＿＿＿＿＿＿＿＿＿＿＿＿＿＿＿＿

A：I see. Any other reasons?

B：Also, [reason]＿＿＿＿＿＿＿＿＿＿＿＿＿＿

A：OK. Thank you for sharing.

B：How about you? What do you think?

A：Actually, I think they should be abolished (too).

or

Actually, I think we should keep them (too).

B：Why?

A：[reason]＿＿＿＿＿＿＿＿＿＿＿＿＿＿＿＿＿＿

COLUMN

　振り袖やスーツを着て集まった新成人たちを祝福する、現在の日本
のような成人式は海外にはありません。
　欧米ではそもそも成人式という発想自体がなく、国によって異なり
ますが、16歳や18歳の誕生日に盛大なパーティーを開いてお祝いす
ることで一人前と見なされます。
　ちなみに、成人として認めてもらうために、ライオンと戦ったり、
サメを素手で捕らえたり、足首に命綱として木のつるを巻いて高い所
から飛び降りたりしなければならない若者たちもいるようです。

24/7 Convenience Stores

今や社会のインフラ（生活の基盤となる施設）ともいわれているコンビニですが、
あなたはコンビニの 24 時間営業について賛成ですか、それとも反対ですか。

Pre-Reading Vocabulary Task

次の語の日本語の意味として最も適切なものを、A～Hから選んで（　　）に記入し
ましょう。

1. indispensable （　　）　　**A.** 不規則な

2. modern （　　）　　**B.** ～を提供する

3. provide ～ （　　）　　**C.** ～に反対する

4. oppose ～ （　　）　　**D.** 暴力的な

5. irregular （　　）　　**E.** 現代の

6. usefulness （　　）　　**F.** 欠くことのできない

7. requirement （　　）　　**G.** 有用性

8. violent （　　）　　**H.** 要求

コンビニは24時間
営業するべきだ

For

1 Convenience stores have become an indispensable part of modern life in Japan. Besides all the delicious snacks and drinks, they provide myriad services at all times of day.

5 2 Some people might oppose it but, in fact, convenience stores should stay open for 24 hours per day for the following reasons.

3 First of all, some people want or need to use convenience stores during the night. They may work irregular hours and convenience stores help to support their hard schedules.

4 Second, all-night convenience stores provide employment 10 opportunities. Believe it or not, there are people who want to work a night shift. Rather than limit job options, society and companies should aim to increase them.

5 Finally, if a convenience store closes down late at night, is it really convenient? Has it not become an "inconvenience store" instead? 15 Without 24/7 opening, a convenience store seems to lose its usefulness.

Against

6 Most of us use convenience stores quite regularly, but do we ever think about the people who run them or who work there?

20 7 With these people in mind, it is proposed that convenience stores should close down late at night for several reasons.

8 Firstly, due to the requirement to stay open 24/7, convenience store workers are suffering. In fact, because of a lack of workers, the store franchise owners themselves must often do the night shift. Many 25 owners are close to exhaustion.

9 Secondly, the hourly pay for the night shift is not enough. Most convenience stores are struggling to break even, so they cannot afford to pay workers more. Rather than underpay workers, they should simply close after midnight.

30 10 Finally, it might be dangerous for workers to work late at night. Sometimes there is only one worker in the store. If a robber becomes violent, there is no backup and so the risk to that worker is too high.

Note

myriad 多様な **per day** 1日（当たり） **all-night** 終夜営業の **employment opportunity** 雇用の機会 **believe it or not** 信じられないかもしれないが **work a night shift** 夜勤をする（= do the night shift） **option** 選択肢 **aim to do** …することを目指す **close down** 閉店する **24/7 opening** 毎日24時間の開店（24/7 は twenty-four hours a day, seven days a week を短くしたもの） **run ~** ～を経営する **with ... in mind** …を念頭において［考慮して］ **store franchise owner** 加盟店のオーナー **exhaustion** 極度の疲労 **hourly pay** 時給 **struggle to break even** 収支が合うように努力する（even は「損得のない」を意味する形容詞） **cannot afford to do** …する余裕がない **underpay ~** ～に十分な賃金を支払わない **robber** 強盗 **backup** 援護してくれる人

Comprehension

次の文は本文の内容を要約したものです。該当する段落の番号を空欄に書き入れて、for または against のどちらに書かれているか○で囲んでください。

1. The salary for this night work is not enough. ☐ for against
2. Staff and owners have to work too hard under this system. ☐ for against
3. A convenience store would become less convenient. ☐ for against
4. The work might be risky, especially for a staff member working alone. ☐ for against
5. By opening all night, people looking for jobs have more options. ☐ for against
6. They provide a useful service, especially for customers who work irregular hours. ☐ for against

Grammar Point 　理由を表す群前置詞

1. due to

*Firstly, **due to** the requirement to stay open 24/7, convenience store workers are suffering.* [第8段落]

2. because of

*In fact, **because of** a lack of workers, the store franchise owners themselves must often do the night shift.* [第8段落]

*1、2ともに「～の理由［せい］で」を意味する。これ以外に on account of や owing to なども使われるが、口語的な because of に対して両方とも文語的。

Writing

以下の例文を参考にしながら、「**～するよりも…するべきだ（できるだろう）**」という表現を学習しましょう。

まずは、本文中の For のセクションから次の文を探してください。

> 1. **Rather than** limit job options, society and companies **should** aim to increase them.

<Rather than+動詞, X should/could+動詞> は、他に取るべき行動があると主張する際に役立つ表現です。Against のセクションにも同様の文があるので探しましょう。

あと2つ例文を挙げておきます。

> 2. **Rather than** close down at night, convenience stores **could** hire foreign workers.
> 3. **Rather than** stay open all night, convenience stores **should** close soon after the last train or bus departs.

それでは賛成か反対の立場を決めた上で、学習した表現を使用しながら、英語で空欄を埋めてみましょう。

FOR : I support the proposal. Rather than ＿＿＿＿＿＿＿＿＿＿＿＿＿

＿＿＿＿＿＿＿＿＿＿＿＿＿＿＿＿＿＿＿＿＿＿＿＿＿＿＿＿＿＿＿

OR

AGAINST : I am against the proposal. Rather than ＿＿＿＿＿＿＿＿＿

＿＿＿＿＿＿＿＿＿＿＿＿＿＿＿＿＿＿＿＿＿＿＿＿＿＿＿＿＿＿＿

Listening Dictation   16

音声を聞いて次の空欄を埋めましょう。

1. When I see a convenience store that is still open late at night, it somehow ¹⁾ (　　　　　) me up and makes me feel ²⁾ (　　　　　).

2. Rather than have staff working all night, ¹⁾ (　　　　) convenience stores with a ²⁾ (　　　　　) system might be better.

3. My two favorite things to buy at the convenience store are ¹⁾ (　　　　　) and ²⁾ (　　　) ³⁾ (　　　　).

24

Speaking

次の会話モデルを使用して、クラスメートや先生にあなたの意見を伝えてみましょう。また、先ほど学習した表現も積極的に使いましょう。

A：Do you agree that convenience stores should stay open 24/7?

B：That's a tough question!

Well, yes, I suppose I agree.

or

Well, no, I think I don't agree.

A：OK. Could I hear your reasons?

B：Sure. [reason]_____

A：I see. Anything else?

B：Also, [reason]_____

A：I got it.

B：How about you? Do you agree that convenience stores should stay open 24/7?

A：Actually, yes, I agree (too).

or

Actually, no, I don't agree (either).

B：Why's that?

A：[reason]_____

コンビニの24時間営業は日本では当たり前ですが、海外ではそうではありません。アジアや米国には日本と同じような営業形態のコンビニが数多く存在しますが、欧州の国々では24時間営業の店舗はあまり見かけません。その背景には、「深夜労働は健康や幸福を侵害する」という国民の考え方が大きく影響しているようです。

ちなみに、フランス国内で初となる24時間営業のコンビニが2018年にパリにオープンして話題を呼びましたが、午後9時以降はすべて自動レジになるそうです。

Unit 6 Japanese Era Names

新天皇の即位に伴い、2019年5月1日から平成に代わる新元号「令和」が導入されました。元号を使用することについてあなたはどう思いますか。

Pre-Reading Vocabulary Task

次の語句の日本語の意味として最も適切なものを、A～Hから選んで（　　）に記入しましょう。

1. exactly	（　）	**A.**	～をやめる、～を取り除く
2. traditional	（　）	**B.**	比較的に
3. whenever ～	（　）	**C.**	途切れることのない
4. reflect ～	（　）	**D.**	伝統的な
5. continuous	（　）	**E.**	～にもかかわらず
6. despite ～	（　）	**F.**	～を反映する
7. get rid of ～	（　）	**G.**	正確に
8. relatively	（　）	**H.**	～するたびに

元号はもう必要ない

 17

 For

1 Japanese era names such as Shōwa, Heisei, Reiwa and so on are no longer necessary and should be phased out of public usage. There are three main reasons to support this suggestion.

2 First, using these era names is confusing for everybody. It is hard to remember exactly when one era began and finished and therefore it is easy to make mistakes. 5

3 Furthermore, the use of traditional era names seems to go against the nature of time. Whenever there is a new monarch in Japan, the year number is reset to one. However, time never resets. A calendar should reflect the continuous progress of time. 10

4 Finally, the usage of Japanese era names can cause trouble at work. For example, it is difficult to calculate someone's age if the date of birth is given using the traditional era name. In a hospital or old people's home, for example, this may hinder the work of the staff. 15

 18

 Against

5 Despite suggestions that we should get rid of the traditional Japanese era names, we should in fact keep this system for the following reasons.

6 First, Japanese era names add color to our lives. People who were born and grew up in the Shōwa era, for example, may have 20 nostalgic memories of that time. Having an era name neatly captures a time period and creates bonds between people from the same era.

7 Second, because the era names change relatively often, we can feel refreshed. A new name for an era seems to indicate a new start for everyone. 25

8 Lastly, it is good to have aspects which are unique to one's country. In this era of globalization, there is a risk of countries losing their identities. It would surely be boring if all countries in the world started to become similar. Let's keep the things which make us unique!

era name 元号、年号（era は「時代」の意味） be no longer ~ もはや~でない be phased out of ~ ~が段階的に廃止される usage 使用 confusing 紛らわしい、混乱させる〔形容詞〕 go against ~ ~に逆らう nature of time 時間の本質 monarch 天皇、君主 old people's home 老人ホーム hinder ~ ~を妨げる add color to ~ ~に彩りを添える nostalgic 懐かしい neatly 適切に time period 期間 bonds 絆 be unique to ~ ~にしかない[特有の] globalization 国際化、グローバル化 identity 独自性、個性 boring 退屈な

Comprehension

次の文は本文の内容を要約したものです。該当する段落の番号を空欄に書き入れて、for または against のどちらに書かれているか○で囲んでください。

1 Japanese era names may make our jobs more difficult.   for   against

2 When a new Japanese era starts, people can get new energy.   for   against

3 Japanese era names are one aspect that helps to make Japan unique.   for   against

4 Japanese era names enrich our lives.   for   against

5 People may be confused by Japanese era names.   for   against

6 It might be unnatural to use a calendar system that sometimes resets the year to one.   for   against

Grammar Point 　動名詞の働き

1. 主語になる

   First, ***using*** these era names is confusing for everybody. [第2段落]

   Having an era name neatly captures a time period... [第6段落]

   *主語のほかに目的語や補語になることもある。

2. 意味上の主語を示す場合

   In this era of globalization, there is a risk of countries ***losing*** their identities. [第8段落]

   *countries が動名詞 losing の意味上の主語になる。

Writing

以下の例文を参考にして、自分の意見を述べる際に役に立つ動詞の使い方を学習しましょう。まずは、本文中の Against のセクションから次の文を探してください。

1. First, Japanese era names **add** color to our lives.

このほかにもよく使用される動詞はたくさんあります。以下がその一例です。

2. Japanese era names
{
   cause
   make us
   help us to
   provide
   seem to
   force us to
   tend to

それでは賛成か反対の立場を決めた上で、下欄の agree か disagree を○で囲み、英語で空欄を埋めてみましょう。なお、上の動詞以外のものを使用しても構いません。

I agree / disagree with this proposal.

Japanese era names _____

_____

Listening Dictation

 19

音声を聞いて次の空欄を埋めましょう。

1. Although [1] (   ) from the Japanese system, other countries also have era names such as the [2] (   ) era in the United Kingdom.

2. Perhaps we could keep the Japanese era system but make it an [1] (   ) system which is only used for [2] (   ) purposes.

3. Foreign people might be [1] (   ) when they first come to Japan and [2] (   ) that two systems for numbering years are used.

Speaking

次の会話モデルを使用して、クラスメートや先生にあなたの意見を伝えてみましょう。また、先ほど学習した表現も積極的に使いましょう。

A：What do you think about the Japanese system of era names?

B：You mean like Heisei and Shōwa?

A：Yes. Do you agree with it or disagree with it?

B：That's a tricky question! I think that I _____ with it.

A：Really? Why's that?

B：[reason]_____

A：I see. Anything else?

B：[reason]_____

A：OK. I understand your position.

B：How about you? What do you think?

A：I (also)_____ with it.

B：OK. Any particular reason?

A：[reason]_____

COLUMN　意外に聞こえるかもしれませんが、今でも元号を使用している国は、日本のほかに台湾と北朝鮮しかありません。サウジアラビアは2016年に「イスラム暦」から西暦に移行しましたし、元号の本家といわれる中国も1911年の辛亥革命で元号を廃止しました。
　現在では世界的にも非常に珍しいこの元号を、今のまま大切に守り続けるのか、あるいは世界の大勢に合わせて廃止するのか。そんなに簡単な問題ではないかもしれません。

Unit 7 Point Cards

ポイントカードはお得な反面、種類の多さなどから敬遠されてしまうことがあります。今あなたの財布にはポイントカードが何枚入っていますか。

Pre-Reading Vocabulary Task

次の語句の日本語の意味として最も適切なものを、A〜Hから選んで（　　）に記入しましょう。

1. accumulate 〜　（　　）　　**A.** 罰

2. wallet　　　　　（　　）　　**B.** 財布

3. unused　　　　　（　　）　　**C.** 〜を手渡す

4. punishment　　　（　　）　　**D.** 〜に記入する

5. local　　　　　　（　　）　　**E.** 〜をため込む

6. convenient　　　（　　）　　**F.** 地元の

7. fill out 〜　　　　（　　）　　**G.** 使われていない

8. hand over 〜　　　（　　）　　**H.** 便利な

ポイントカードはいらない

 20

For

[1] Over time, most people accumulate several point cards from stores.

[2] Check your own wallet right now... you might be surprised at how many you have.

[3] Although we may have many point cards, they are not good for the following reasons.

[4] Firstly, as mentioned above, people tend to accumulate point cards. In fact, we get so many that they clutter up our wallets. Some people's wallets are almost bulging with unused point cards.

[5] Secondly, to be honest, many point systems are stingy. Even if you get some points, the discount obtained when you use them is minuscule. It would be better if the shops just made their goods a little cheaper in the first place.

[6] Finally, we often get point cards for shops which we rarely visit. By the time we visit the shop again, the points have expired. Somehow it feels like a punishment for not going to that shop often.

 21

Against

[7] Point cards are popular and indeed useful, both for customers and stores.

[8] There are several reasons for this.

[9] Firstly, point cards are great to have for shops that we visit often. A good example is a local supermarket. If it is in a convenient location, we may visit such a shop once a week or more. In this situation, the points accumulate quickly.

[10] The second reason is connected to the first. There are shops such as the aforementioned supermarket that we have to visit. Even if there were no point card system, we would go there. Thus, the points can be seen as a kind of bonus.

[11] Lastly, point cards are very easy to use. We do not have to fill out a form or scan a QR-code or something like that. We just hand over the card and get points or redeem points. It is simple, quick and, because the card is always in our wallet, we can do it every time we visit the shop.

Note

over time 時間の経過と共に **as mentioned above** 上に述べたように **clutter up ~** ~をいっぱいにする **bulge with ~** ~でぱんぱんに膨れる **to be honest** 正直に言って **stingy** けちな **minuscule** ほんのわずかの **in the first place** 初めから **expire** 期限が切れる **somehow** 何だか、何となく **aforementioned** 前述の **a kind of ~** 一種の~ **form** 用紙 **scan ~** ~を読み取る **something like that** そのようなこと **redeem ~** ~を現金［商品］に換える **every time** ~するたびに〔接続詞的〕

Comprehension

次の文は本文の内容を要約したものです。該当する段落の番号を空欄に書き入れて、for または against のどちらに書かれているか○で囲んでください。

1 Our wallets or purses get filled up with point cards. [ ] for against

2 It is easy to use point cards. [ ] for against

3 A point system is an extra benefit if we visit the shop often. [ ] for against

4 We collect points quickly at shops we visit often. [ ] for against

5 Points cannot be redeemed if we rarely visit the shop. [ ] for against

6 Point systems only give us a tiny reward. [ ] for against

Grammar Point so … that ~

*In fact, we get **so** many **that** they clutter up our wallets.* ［第4段落］

*so の直後に形容詞や副詞などを置いて「とても…なので~」や「~なほど…」という意味を表す。このほかに同じ意味を表すものとして**<such+(a/an+) 形容詞+名詞+that~>**がある。なお、両方とも口語体では that が省略されることが多い。

例1) I'm so tired (that) I can't walk any more.

例2) I got such a nice present (that) I couldn't get to sleep.
  = I got so nice a present (that) I couldn't get to sleep.

33

Writing

次の例文を参考にしながら、「**もし～なら…だろうに**」という仮定法の表現を学習しましょう。
まずは、本文中の For のセクションから以下の文を探してください。

1. **It would be better if** the shops just **made** their goods a little cheaper in the first place.

<If＋主語＋動詞の過去形、主語＋would＋動詞の原形> の形をとる仮定法過去は、現在の事実とは反対の仮定を表す表現で、議論の場でも使用されます。Against のセクションにも同様のものがあるので確認しましょう。

他の例文も紹介しておきます。

2. **If I were** a store owner, **I would** definitely set up a point card system.
3. **If I had** no point cards, my wallet **would be** much slimmer.

それでは賛成か反対の立場を決めた上で、学習した表現を使用しながら、英語で空欄を埋めてみましょう。

FOR： Point cards are not good. _____

_____

OR

AGAINST： Point cards are good. _____

_____

Listening Dictation

 22

音声を聞いて次の空欄を埋めましょう。

1. Some stores now use ¹⁾(　　　　　) instead of ²⁾(　　　　　) point cards.

2. Most point cards are very ¹⁾(　　　　　) so I do not think they take up too much ²⁾(　　　　) in my wallet.

3. I do not know why but it seems that point cards are more commonly used in ¹⁾(　　　　) than ²⁾(　　　　).

Speaking

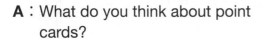

次の会話モデルを使用して、クラス
メートや先生にあなたの意見を伝え
てみましょう。また、先ほど学習した
表現も積極的に使いましょう。

A：What do you think about point
cards?

B：Point cards? I don't think they are so good.

or

Point cards? I think they are good.

A：Really? Why is that?

B：Well, [reason]_____

A：OK. Any other reasons?

B：Also, [reason]_____

A：I see.

B：How about you? What do you think about point cards?

A：Well, I (also) think they are not so good.

or

Well, I (also) think they are good.

B：OK. Any reasons?

A：Yes. [reasons]_____

　2017年に実施されたある調査によると、普段からためているポイ
ントカードのベスト３は以下の通りでした。
　　1位　Tポイント　62.7%
　　2位　家電量販店のポイント　42.1%
　　3位　楽天ポイント　41.7%
　ちなみに、男女別で大きな差が見られたのは、ドラッグストアのポ
イント（29.1%差）とスーパーマーケットのポイント（23.7%差）で、
いずれも女性の方の割合が高かったそうです。

Unit 8 Disaster Volunteers

地震などの自然災害が起きると欠かせないのがボランティアの存在です。現在彼らに報酬は支払われていませんが、この点についてあなたはどう思いますか。

Pre-Reading Vocabulary Task

次の語の日本語の意味として最も適切なものを、A～Hから選んで（　　）に記入しましょう。

1. ordinary	（　）	**A.**	～を操作する
2. donate ～	（　）	**B.**	～を寄付する
3. serve ～	（　）	**C.**	マイナスの、否定的な
4. operate ～	（　）	**D.**	普通の
5. spirit	（　）	**E.**	報酬
6. negative	（　）	**F.**	～を出す、～に給仕する
7. consequence	（　）	**G.**	精神
8. reward	（　）	**H.**	結果

政府は災害ボランティアに報酬を支払うべきだ

CD 23

1 A natural disaster is without doubt a terrible thing. However, one good thing is the response of ordinary people. Many people donate money or items and also volunteer to help.

2 Although people volunteer for free, it is clear that the government should in fact pay them. Please consider the following points. 5

3 First, these people are doing work for the government. Removing debris, cleaning up streets and homes, serving food and more... all of these tasks are the responsibility of the government.

4 Second, the work that volunteers do is grueling and can even be dangerous. They may be lifting heavy objects, using tools, operating machines and working long hours. For people making such a great effort, a payment is deserved. 10

5 Finally, when a disaster happens, some local government employees and others do the same work as volunteers but get paid for it. Surely it is unfair to pay one group of people but not the other. 15

CD 24

6 In regard to disasters, some people have suggested that payment should be made to volunteers.

7 However, this is not appropriate for the following reasons.

8 First, humans naturally want to help people in need or people who are suffering. Whether family, friends or even strangers, when we see somebody in trouble, we want to help and we do not expect payment. This is the spirit of volunteering. 20

9 Second, if the government pays people to do relief work, it may have some negative consequences. For example, fewer and fewer people may offer to volunteer because they expect that the work is being done by paid workers. 25

10 Finally, the reward for helping people is not money but the knowledge that those people can return to a normal life. By helping people we nurture our mind and our soul... that alone is worth more than any salary. 30

natural disaster 自然災害　volunteer to do …しようと進んで申し出る　for free ただで〔口語〕　debris がれき　grueling きつい　deserved 当然の　local government employee 地方公務員　and others …など　in regard to ~ ~に関しては　people in need 困っている人々（need は名詞で「困った事態」の意味、somebody in trouble は「困っている人」を意味する）　relief work 救援活動　fewer and fewer people do …する人がますます少なくなる　paid worker 有給の労働者　nurture ~ ~を育む　alone〔名詞・代名詞の後に置いて〕…だけでも

Comprehension

次の文は本文の内容を要約したものです。該当する段落の番号を空欄に書き入れて、for または against のどちらに書かれているか◯で囲んでください。

❶ Volunteer work is actually the government's responsibility.　　　　☐　　for　　against

❷ Some people get paid for the same work.　　　　☐　　for　　against

❸ Paying people may reduce the number of people who help.　　　　☐　　for　　against

❹ It is tough work and deserves a reward.　　　　☐　　for　　against

❺ The feeling of having helped people is a reward in itself.　　　　☐　　for　　against

❻ Volunteers want to help and expect no payment.　　　　☐　　for　　against

Grammar Point さまざまな受動態

1. get を用いた受動態

　… *some local government employees and others* … ***get paid*** *for it.*
　[第5段落]

　　＊受動態には「動作（～される）」を表す場合と「状態（～された状態にある）」を表す場合がある。主に口語では、動作を表す受動態に get がよく使われる。

2. 助動詞を用いた受動態

　… *payment **should be made** to volunteers.* [第6段落]

3. 進行形の受動態

　… *the work **is being done** by paid workers.* [第9段落]

　　＊＜be 動詞＋being＋過去分詞＞で「～されているところだ」を意味する。

Writing

以下の例文を参考にしながら、「**〜の時には…したい**」という表現を学習しましょう。まずは、本文中の Against のセクションから次の文を探してください。

1. Whether family, friends or even strangers, **when** we see somebody in trouble, we **want to** help...

他の例文も紹介しておきます。参考にしてください。

2. **When** a disaster happens, people **want to** donate money.
3. **When** I make a great effort, I **want to** get paid.

それでは賛成か反対の立場を決めた上で、学習した表現を使用しながら、英語で空欄を埋めてみましょう。

FOR : When _____ , _____ want to

_____

OR

AGAINST : When _____ , _____ want to

_____

Listening Dictation

音声を聞いて次の空欄を埋めましょう。

CD 25

1. ¹⁾ (   ) I have never volunteered myself, I greatly ²⁾ (   ) people who do so.

2. If a ¹⁾ (   ) were made for volunteering, the ²⁾ (   ) would have to check that everybody is actually doing the work.

3. The payment need not be ¹⁾ (   ). It could be local ²⁾ (   ) from the disaster-stricken area, for example.

Speaking

次の会話モデルを使用して、クラスメートや先生にあなたの意見を伝えてみましょう。また、先ほど学習した表現も積極的に使いましょう。

A：Do you think that disaster volunteers should receive payment from the government?

B：Well, yes, I do.

　　or

　　Well, actually, no, I don't.

A：OK. Could you explain why?

B：Sure. First, [reason]_____

　　Also, [reason]_____

A：I see.

B：How about you? What do you think?

A：I (also) think they should be paid.

　　or

　　I don't think they should be paid, (either).

B：Why's that?

A：[reason]_____

　　And also [reason]_____

　　今回のテーマの参考になりそうな組織が、洪水被害に悩まされているドイツにあります。
　　内務省が所管するTHW（連邦技術支援隊）という組織で、国家予算から年間200億円が支出されています。構成員の99%がボランティア救援隊員（約8万人）で、研修を含め年間120時間の勤務が義務付けられていますが、活動後に申請すれば実費や小遣い程度のお金が支給されます。彼らは、2011年の東日本大震災の時にも日本に派遣されて救援活動に加わったそうです。

Unit 9 Domestic Trip vs. Abroad

国際ターミナル　　　国内ターミナル

若者の「旅行離れ」が指摘されていますが、皆さんはよく旅行をしますか。もしどこにでも行けるとしたら、国内旅行と海外旅行どちらに興味がありますか。

Pre-Reading Vocabulary Task

次の語の日本語の意味として最も適切なものを、A～Hから選んで（　　）に記入しましょう。

1. trip	（　）	**A.** めったに…しない
2. domestic	（　）	**B.** おそらく
3. international	（　）	**C.** 国内の、家庭の
4. probably	（　）	**D.** 面白い、おかしな
5. scenery	（　）	**E.** 旅行
6. fascinating	（　）	**F.** 海外の、国際的な
7. rarely	（　）	**G.** 景色
8. funny	（　）	**H.** 魅力的な

10万円あったら海外旅行よりも国内旅行だ

 26

For

[1] If you had 100,000 yen and wanted to use it to take a trip somewhere, where would you go? Although it is fun to think of possible destinations, the first thing to decide is whether to take a domestic trip or an international one.

[2] For several reasons, a domestic trip is surely the best bet.

[3] First and above all, it is much easier to take a trip within Japan than to travel overseas. There will be no problems with speaking a foreign language, no currency to change and the food will definitely be palatable.

[4] Second, think about safety. Although most tourist spots overseas are probably not dangerous, Japan is known as being a particularly safe country. Simply put, we can travel in Japan with peace of mind.

[5] And last but not least, a tour in Japan is a good chance to find out more about Japan's deep culture and long history. Each prefecture offers something interesting. In fact, the only problem is choosing where to go!

 27

Against

[6] It cannot be denied that a domestic trip is good. After all, Japan is famous for its beautiful scenery, nice food and safety.

[7] However, an international trip is by far the better choice for young people for the following reasons.

[8] First, traveling overseas broadens our horizons. If we always stay within our comfort zone, we do not develop. Going abroad, meeting foreign people, seeing foreign places and trying new things give us a new perspective.

[9] Second, on a trip overseas, everything seems so fresh and different. All the sights and sounds, all the places, even small things such as the items on sale in a supermarket... everything is new and fascinating.

[10] Finally, we Japanese have spent years studying English but rarely get a chance to speak it. A trip abroad is a great chance to use English for real communication. And even if there is a miscommunication, no problem! That will make a funny story to tell friends back in Japan.

Note

destination 行き先　**the best bet** 一番のお薦め、最善の策（bet は「選ぶべき方策」の意味）
currency 通貨　**palatable** 口に合う　**tourist spot** 観光地　**simply put** 簡単に言えば（= to
put it simply）　**with peace of mind** 安心して　**last but not least** 大事なことを言い忘れたが
prefecture 県　**it cannot be denied that ~** ~は否定できない　**after all**〔前文への理由や
説明を示して〕何しろ…だから　**by far**〔比較級を強めて〕はるかに　**broaden one's horizons**
視野を広げる（horizon は「地平線」の意味）　**comfort zone** 安全地帯、居心地の良い領域
perspective 物の見方　**item on sale** 特売品　**miscommunication** コミュニケーションの
行き違い

Comprehension

次の文は本文の内容を要約したものです。該当する段落の番号を空欄に書き入れて、
for または against のどちらに書かれているか○で囲んでください。

❶ For this option, safety is guaranteed. 　　　　　　□　　for　　against

❷ Everything will be different from what we are used to. 　　□　　for　　against

❸ Traveling will be easy and smooth. 　　　　　　□　　for　　against

❹ There is a chance to speak English in real situations. 　　□　　for　　against

❺ We can learn about our own culture and history. 　　□　　for　　against

❻ We can discover new horizons. 　　　　　　□　　for　　against

Grammar Point 　　　　疑問詞 ＋ to 不定詞

1. *... the first thing to decide is __whether to__ take a domestic trip or an international one.*［第1段落］

2. *In fact, the only problem is choosing __where to__ go!*［第5段落］

*「疑問詞の意味 ＋ ～すべきか」の意味になる。このほかに what, who, when, how
などの疑問詞を to 不定詞の直前に置くことができるが、why to という形はない。

例1）I'm still thinking what to do next.

例2）Have you decided who to vote for?

例3）Nobody knows when to get off this train.

例4）Could you tell me how to get to the library?

Writing

以下の例文を参考にしながら、「〜するのに良い機会だ」という表現を学習しましょう。まずは、本文中の For のセクションから次の文を探してください。

1. And last but not least, a tour in Japan **is a good chance to** find out more about Japan's deep culture and long history.

<A is a good/great chance [opportunity] to do> という表現は、ある行動によって絶好の機会がもたらされる、という事実を伝えるときに役立ちます。Against のセクションにも同様の文があるので探してみましょう。

この他にも例文を2つ挙げておきます。

2. Traveling in Japan **is a good opportunity to** visit friends' hometowns.
3. Taking a trip overseas **is a great chance to** buy brand-name items at low prices.

それでは賛成か反対の立場を決めた上で、学習した表現を使用しながら、英語で空欄を埋めてみましょう。

FOR： If I had 100,000 yen for a trip, I would travel domestically. A trip in Japan _____

OR

AGAINST： If I had 100,000 yen for a trip, I would travel internationally. A trip overseas _____

Listening Dictation

 CD 28

音声を聞いて次の空欄を埋めましょう。

1. Thanks to low-cost ¹⁾(　　　　　), in some cases it might actually be ²⁾(　　　　) to travel abroad than to travel inside Japan.

2. Thanks to ¹⁾(　　　　) buses, it is now possible to travel inside Japan at very ²⁾(　　　　　) prices.

3. Whether traveling inside Japan or traveling abroad, your trip will be a good chance to take lots of photographs to ¹⁾(　　　　) to ²⁾(　　　　　).

Speaking

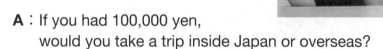

次の会話モデルを使用して、クラス
メートや先生にあなたの意見を伝え
てみましょう。また、先ほど学習した
表現も積極的に使いましょう。

A：If you had 100,000 yen,
would you take a trip inside Japan or overseas?

B：I would probably take a trip in Japan.

　　or

　　I would probably travel overseas.

A：That's interesting. What are your reasons?

B：Well, [reason]_____

A：OK. I see.

B：Also, [reason]_____

A：I see.

B：How about you? Which would you choose?

A：Actually, I would probably travel in Japan (too).

　　or

　　Actually, I would probably travel overseas (too).

B：Why's that?

A：[reason]_____

　　大学生にとって一番の旅行は卒業旅行かもしれません。そこで卒業
旅行に関するさまざまなアンケート調査を調べたところ、意外な結果
が見つかりました。
　　ある総合旅行サイトが、卒業旅行に行った経験のある社会人1年目
の男女400人に、旅行先の条件として「インスタ映え」する場所であ
ることを重視したかどうか尋ねたところ、「はい」と答えた女性は全体
の15%にすぎませんでした。これに対し、「インスタ映え」を意識し
ていた男性の数は予想以上に多く、およそ2倍の27%にも上ること
が分かりました。

Unit 10 Studying English Abroad

語学留学といえばかつては米国やオーストラリアが一般的でしたが、最近ではフィリピンの人気が高まっています。留学するならあなたはどの国がいいですか。

Pre-Reading Vocabulary Task

次の語の日本語の意味として最も適切なものを、A〜Hから選んで（　　）に記入しましょう。

1. furthermore	（　）	**A.**	（料金などが）手頃な
2. reasonable	（　）	**B.**	従って、それゆえに
3. predict 〜	（　）	**C.**	見慣れた、よく知られた
4. nevertheless	（　）	**D.**	〜を予測する、〜を予言する
5. support 〜	（　）	**E.**	〜を支持する
6. suitable	（　）	**F.**	それでもやはり、それにもかかわらず
7. familiar	（　）	**G.**	さらに
8. therefore	（　）	**H.**	適切な

英語を勉強するなら米国よりもフィリピンだ

CD 29

For

[1] About 20 years ago, most Japanese students who studied English abroad went to the United States, Australia or Britain. However, these days many people study English in Asian countries, such as the Philippines.

[2] In fact, this is a better option for the following reasons.　5

[3] First, it is easier and cheaper to visit the Philippines. The flight time is under five hours and, by using a low-cost carrier, we can find tickets for under 40,000 yen. Furthermore, tuition, food and accommodations are very reasonable, too.

[4] Secondly, the English teachers in the Philippines are Asian, the　10 same as we Japanese. We can feel a sense of affinity with them and, on a cultural level, it is easier to communicate with them.

[5] Finally, have you heard the expression, "the Asian Century"? Experts predict that, in the 21st century, Asia will become the center of global business. Many Japanese business people will need to speak　15 English with other Asian people in the future. Thus, an Asian teacher of English is the best choice.

CD 30

Against

[6] Destinations for study abroad have certainly increased in recent years. Nevertheless, for students who wish to brush up their English ability, the United States is still the best option.　20

[7] There are several reasons to support this point of view.

[8] First of all, we Japanese study American English at school. The language presented in our textbooks is American English and the listening exercises are spoken with an American accent. Thus, the most suitable place for further study is surely the United States.　25

[9] Secondly, the United States offers a comfortable and even familiar setting for study. For example, many parts of the country have four seasons, providing an environment similar to that of Japan. And we also have a good idea of the American lifestyle through watching movies and TV dramas.　30

[10] Finally, teachers in the United States may have the latest techniques and technology for teaching languages. Therefore, students can learn efficiently.

Unit 10

47

Comprehension

次の文は本文の内容を要約したものです。該当する段落の番号を空欄に書き入れて、
for または against のどちらに書かれているか○で囲んでください。

1 We can study in a comfortable and familiar environment.　　[　]　for　against

2 We can feel close to the teachers.　　[　]　for　against

3 We can study the same type of English that we have learned so far.　　[　]　for　against

4 This option is the best in terms of price and convenience.　　[　]　for　against

5 The instructors and learning environment may be the most advanced.　　[　]　for　against

6 We can study the kind of English that we will most likely have to use in the future.　　[　]　for　against

Grammar Point 　　付帯状況の分詞構文

*For example, many parts of the country have four seasons, **providing** an environment similar to that of Japan.* ［第9段落］

＊分詞構文の中で最もよく用いられるのが付帯状況を表す分詞構文で、これは「動作の
連続（～して、そして）」と「動作の同時（～しながら）」に分類される。付帯状況のほ
かに、「時（～すると）」・「理由（～なので）」・「条件（～ならば）」・「譲歩（～だけれども）」
の意味を表す場合もある。なお、上の文は付帯状況の動作の連続を表す分詞構文。

　例1）The train starts soon, arriving in Kyoto at ten. ［動作の連続］

　例2）The students were walking to the station talking to each other. ［動作
　　　の同時］

Writing

以下の例文を参考にしながら、「**だから…だ**」という表現を学習しましょう。
まずは、本文中の For のセクションから次の文を探してください。

1. Many Japanese business people will need to speak English with other Asian people in the future. **Thus**, an Asian teacher of English is the best choice.

あることを主張した直後に **Thus** を用いると、全体の説得力が増します。Against のセクションにも同様の文があるので探してみましょう。

あと2つ例文を追加します。なお、**Thus** の代わりに **Therefore** を使うこともできます。

2. Online lessons with Philippine teachers are popular now. **Thus**, studying in the Philippines makes sense.
3. The United States has many immigrants who must study English. **Therefore**, the teachers there have a lot of experience.

それでは賛成か反対の立場を決めた上で、学習した表現を使用しながら、英語で空欄を埋めてみましょう。

```
FOR : [assertion] _____

        Thus, _____

OR

AGAINST : [assertion] _____

        Thus, _____
```

Listening Dictation

 31

音声を聞いて次の空欄を埋めましょう。

1. [1) (   ) is another country in Asia that is becoming [2)] (   ) as a good place to learn English.

2. English is the language of global [1)] (   ) and thus students need to get used to many different [2)] (   ) of spoken English.

3. When studying abroad, rather than the [1)] (   ), perhaps the most [2)] (   ) thing is using English a lot, both inside and outside the classroom.

Speaking

次の会話モデルを使用して、クラスメートや先生にあなたの意見を伝えてみましょう。また、先ほど学習した表現も積極的に使いましょう。

A：Which do you think is better, studying English in the Philippines or studying English in the United States?

B：I think studying English in the Philippines/the United States is probably the best choice.

A：Really? How come?

B：Well, [reason]＿＿＿＿＿＿＿＿＿＿＿＿＿＿＿＿＿＿＿＿＿＿

A：Sure. Any other reasons?

B：Also, [reason]＿＿＿＿＿＿＿＿＿＿＿＿＿＿＿＿＿＿＿＿＿＿

A：I see.

B：How about you? Which do you think is the best option?

A：Actually, I think the Philippines is the best choice (too).

or

Actually, I think the United States is the best choice (too).

B：Why's that?

A：[reason]＿＿＿＿＿＿＿＿＿＿＿＿＿＿＿＿＿＿＿＿＿＿＿＿＿＿

　　自宅でスカイプを使用して現地の講師と英語で会話するオンライン英会話の世界でも、フィリピン人講師の存在は今や欠かせません。その最大の理由が、ネイティブの半額以下という人件費の安さにありますが、彼らのフレンドリーな国民性、そして日本との時差がわずか1時間であることも大いに関係しているようです。一昔前は英会話学校に通うのに月何万円もかかりましたが、フィリピン人講師のおかげで、今では安いところだと1レッスン（25分）150円以下で受講できるそうです。

Unit 11 More Foreign Visitors

旅行者数

インバウンド

年

日本を訪れる外国人観光客の数は増え続けていますが、その一方で無視できない問題も生じているようです。外国人観光客を今後も増やしていくべきだと思いますか。

Pre-Reading Vocabulary Task

次の語句の日本語の意味として最も適切なものを、A～Hから選んで（　　）に記入しましょう。

1. introduce ～　　（　　）　　**A.** 消費（量）

2. the latter　　（　　）　　**B.** 現在の

3. population　　（　　）　　**C.** 後者（の）

4. consumption　　（　　）　　**D.** ～を紹介する

5. current　　（　　）　　**E.** 住民、市民

6. citizen　　（　　）　　**F.** ～に頼る

7. unstable　　（　　）　　**G.** 人口

8. rely on ～　　（　　）　　**H.** 不安定な

外国人観光客の数を 今後も増やしていくべきだ

 32

For

[1] The number of foreign visitors to Japan has skyrocketed in recent years. Tourist spots in Japan are teeming with people from all over the world.

[2] In keeping with this trend, Japan should aim to increase the number of foreign visitors from now on. Please consider the following reasons.

[3] First, sharing Japanese culture with the world is a wonderful thing. Intercultural exchange is a two-way street—we learn about other cultures and introduce our own. The best way to do the latter is to welcome more and more foreign visitors to Japan.

[4] Second, increased numbers of inbound tourists have a positive effect on the economy. Due to the low birthrate, the Japanese population is decreasing and thus consumption will also decrease. More foreign tourists can mitigate this.

[5] Finally, an increase in foreign tourists will actually help to preserve Japanese culture. For example, foreign visitors want to see traditional Japanese places and culture, try traditional Japanese food and buy traditional Japanese products.

 33

Against

[6] It is nice to meet people from other countries and have cross-cultural exchange with them. However, in the case of inbound tourists, every country must set a limit on numbers. Accordingly, Japan should not increase the number of foreign visitors from now on. There are several reasons.

[7] First, the services in our cities are already at breaking point with the current number of tourists. For example, trains and buses are packed with people. Citizens in some areas have trouble continuing their daily activities.

[8] Second, welcoming more foreign visitors drives up prices for everybody. Things such as hotel rooms are becoming very expensive. When citizens need to use a hotel, they may not be able to find something affordable.

[9] Finally, tourism is an unstable sector of the economy. For example, after the 3/11 disaster, tourism suddenly dropped. Instead of increasing tourists and relying on tourism, we should encourage other economic sectors.

Note

skyrocket 急激に増加する〔口語〕 **teem with ~** ～であふれる **in keeping with ~** ～に合わせて **from now on** 今後 **intercultural exchange** 異文化交流（= cross-cultural exchange） **two-way street** 互恵的関係（本来は「2車線道路」の意味） **inbound tourist** 外国からやって来る旅行者（inbound は「本国行きの」の意味） **have a positive effect on ~** ～にプラスの効果を及ぼす **birthrate** 出生率 **mitigate ~** ～を緩和する **set a limit on ~** ～に制限を設ける **accordingly** 従って **be at breaking point with ~** ～でもう限界だ（breaking point は「限界点」の意味） **be packed with ~** ～でいっぱいだ **have trouble doing** …するのに苦労する **drive up ~** ～をつり上げる **affordable**（料金が）手頃な **tourism** 観光産業 **sector** 部門 **the 3/11 disaster** 3月11日の大災害

Comprehension

次の文は本文の内容を要約したものです。該当する段落の番号を空欄に書き入れて、for または against のどちらに書かれているか○で囲んでください。

1 The number of visitors is already putting a strain on our services. ☐ for against

2 More visitors means increased prices. ☐ for against

3 Increasing foreign visitors will benefit the economy. ☐ for against

4 Income from tourism is not steady in the long term. ☐ for against

5 Foreign tourists help to maintain our traditional culture. ☐ for against

6 We can introduce Japanese culture to more and more people. ☐ for against

Grammar Point something ＋ 形容詞

*When citizens need to use a hotel, they may not be able to find **something affordable**.* ［第8段落］

* something のような –thing が付く代名詞を修飾するとき、形容詞は後ろに置かれる。–one が付く代名詞（someone など）や、-body が付く代名詞（somebody など）も同様。

例1）These reports tell us nothing new.

例2）Have you ever met someone famous?

Writing

以下の例文を参考にしながら、「**例えば…**」という表現を学習しましょう。
まずは、本文中の For のセクションから次の文を探してください。

1. Finally, an increase in foreign tourists will actually help to preserve Japanese culture. **For example,** foreign visitors want to see traditional Japanese places and culture...

議論の場で、ある主張をした直後に **<For example, ...>** と例示すると、情報をさらに盛り込むことができるだけでなく、相手に自分の主張をより理解してもらいやすくなります。Against のセクションにも同様の文が2つあるので探してみましょう。

例文を2つ紹介します。参考にしてください。

2. Increased tourism is good for the economy. **For example,** tourists buy lots of souvenirs.
3. Increased tourism might be bad for the environment. **For example,** more buses for tourists will mean more CO_2 emissions.

それでは賛成か反対の立場を決めた上で、学習した表現を使用しながら、英語で空欄を埋めてみましょう。

FOR : Increased tourism is _____

        For example, _____

OR

AGAINST : Increased tourism is _____

        For example, _____

Listening Dictation

 34

音声を聞いて次の空欄を埋めましょう。

1. Foreign visitors with large [1] (   ) can be a problem on a crowded train but, on the other hand, they have to get to and from the [2] (   ).

2. I hope to get a job [1] (   ) with tourism after graduation so of course I am studying [2] (   ) as hard as I can.

3. Although more tourists are coming to Japan, I heard on the news that the number of Japanese people traveling [1] (   ) is also [2] (   ).

Speaking

次の会話モデルを使用して、クラス
メートや先生にあなたの意見を伝え
てみましょう。また、先ほど学習した
表現も積極的に使いましょう。

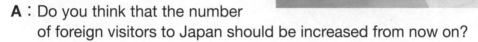

A：Do you think that the number
of foreign visitors to Japan should be increased from now on?

B：Yes, I do.

　　or

　　No, I don't.

A：I see. Why do you think that way?

B：Well, [reason]_____

A：Anything else?

B：Also, [reason]_____

A：OK. Thank you for telling me your opinion.

B：How about you? What do you think?

A：Actually, I (also) think that we should increase the number of foreign
tourists.

　　or

　　Actually, I (also) think we should not increase the number of foreign
tourists.

B：OK. Why's that?

A：[reason]_____

　　皆さんは「観光公害」や「オーバーツーリズム」といった言葉をご存
知でしょうか。ある１カ所の観光地に観光客が大量に押し寄せること
で、住民の日常生活に支障が出る状態を指す言葉です。
　　すでに京都では大きな問題になっていて、二条城の開門時間を通常
より早くしたり、京都の中でまだ認知度の低い観光スポットをアピー
ルしたり、春の桜や秋の紅葉以外に「初夏の青（葉の）もみじ」を宣伝
して、何とか観光客の分散を図ろうと努力しています。観光による収
入は市の財政の１つの柱でもあるため、京都市にとってこの問題は実
に頭の痛いものであることは間違いなさそうです。

Unit 12 New Year's Eve Fireworks

最近では、小規模ながら「年越しカウントダウン花火大会」が国内でも実施されるようになりました。大みそかに大規模な花火大会を行うことについてあなたはどう思いますか。

Pre-Reading Vocabulary Task

次の語句の日本語の意味として最も適切なものを、A〜Hから選んで（　　）に記入しましょう。

1. advertisement （　） **A.** 〜を共有する

2. share 〜 （　） **B.** 世代

3. encourage 〜 （　） **C.** 言うまでもなく、明らかに

4. generation （　） **D.** 〜にこだわる、〜に固執する

5. obviously （　） **E.** 一般に

6. generally （　） **F.** 〜を励ます

7. aspect （　） **G.** 側面

8. stick to 〜 （　） **H.** 宣伝、広告

日本も「年越しカウントダウン花火大会」を開催するべきだ

 35

For

[1] Every year at midnight on December 31st, cities around the world put on huge firework displays to welcome in the New Year. Sydney, Hong Kong, Dubai, London, New York, and more, all have major firework displays.

[2] Japan, on the other hand, only has minor displays at New Year. 5 Perhaps we should change this for the following reasons.

[3] First of all, a major firework display in Tokyo (or another city) would be a fantastic advertisement for Japan. Such a display would make the news around the world and raise the profile of Japan on the world stage. 10

[4] In addition, Japan has a wonderful "firework culture." Over hundreds of years, firework technology has been greatly developed in Japan. A major display at New Year would be a great chance to share this culture with the world.

[5] Finally, a huge firework display is a fun and inspiring way to start 15 the New Year, especially for young people. Let's have a major New Year's display to cheer up and encourage the younger generation.

 36

Against

[6] Most people like firework displays and obviously there is no problem with that. However, a major New Year's firework display in Tokyo or another Japanese city is not needed for 20 the following reasons.

[7] The first point is that the Japanese traditional New Year is generally quiet and solemn. We do things such as praying at a shrine or ringing a temple bell. A noisy firework display does not fit in with these beautiful traditions. 25

[8] Furthermore, a major New Year's firework display would attract huge crowds of people. Roads would be closed and public transportation congested. This would surely obstruct people who want to visit a shrine at midnight, for example.

[9] Finally, in Japan, summer is the time to hold major firework 30 displays. Both Japanese people and foreign visitors enjoy this aspect of the Japanese summer. Let's stick to summer firework displays to keep our traditions.

Comprehension

次の文は本文の内容を要約したものです。該当する段落の番号を空欄に書き入れて、for または against のどちらに書かれているか○で囲んでください。

1 We can share our culture with people in other countries.　☐　for　against

2 It might make young people happy and enthusiastic about the coming year.　☐　for　against

3 It would help to publicize Japan's good points.　☐　for　against

4 We should protect our usual firework customs.　☐　for　against

5 It would cause a lot of trouble for people doing other activities.　☐　for　against

6 It would not match our existing New Year's traditions.　☐　for　against

Grammar Point 　　such の用法

1. such a/an ＋ 名詞：そのような～ / このような～

***Such** a display would make the news around the world ...* ［第3段落］

　　＊such の後に数えられない名詞を置くこともできる。

　　例）Such weather is very unusual in Tokyo.

2. A such as B：B のような A （= such A as B）

*We do things **such as** praying at a shrine or ringing a temple bell.* ［第7段落］

　　＊上の文は ＜such A as B＞ を使って以下のように書き換えることができる。

　　= We do **such** things **as** praying at a shrine or ringing a temple bell.

58

Writing

以下の例文を参考にしながら、「**～するために…しよう**」という表現を学習しましょう。まずは、本文中の For のセクションから次の文を探してください。

1. **Let's** have a major New Year's display **to** cheer up and encourage the younger generation.

<Let's do X to do Y>という表現は、ある特定の行動がどんな目的を果たす助けになるのか、ということを説明するときに役立ちます。Against のセクションにも同様の文があります。確認しましょう。

このほかに２つ例文を載せておきます。

2. **Let's** hold a firework display around Tokyo Sky Tree **to** show off our interesting buildings.
3. **Let's** advertise our ancient New Year's traditions **to** attract more foreign tourists.

それでは賛成か反対の立場を決めた上で、学習した表現を使用しながら、英語で空欄を埋めてみましょう。

FOR : I support the proposal. Let's _____

_____

OR

AGAINST : I am against the proposal. Let's _____

_____

Listening Dictation

 37

音声を聞いて次の空欄を埋めましょう。

1. Due to time differences, the first major New Year firework display is held in
   ¹⁾ (　　　　) and the last major one is probably the ²⁾ (　　　　) display.

2. Big cities such as Tokyo might not have enough ¹⁾ (　　　) to
   ²⁾ (　　　) both summer firework displays and also a major New Year's display.

3. A major New Year's firework display might be good for local ¹⁾ (　　　) which could ²⁾ (　　　) lots of snacks and drinks to passers-by.

Speaking

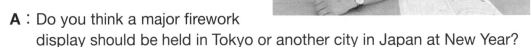

次の会話モデルを使用して、クラスメートや先生にあなたの意見を伝えてみましょう。また、先ほど学習した表現も積極的に使いましょう。

A：Do you think a major firework
display should be held in Tokyo or another city in Japan at New Year?

B：That's an interesting question.

Well, yes, I do.

or

Well, no, I don't.

A：OK. Could you give your reasons?

B：Sure. [reason]_____

A：I see. Anything else?

B：[reason]_____

A：Thanks for sharing your opinion.

B：How about you? What do you think?

A：Actually, I think we should have one (too).

or

Actually, I don't think we need one (either).

B：I see. Why do you think that way?

A：[reason]_____

 　本文中にも少し触れられていましたが、ドバイのカウントダウン花火大会はその桁外れの豪華さで知られています。中でも2014年から2015年にかけての花火大会では、新年の祝砲としてたった6分間で50万発もの花火が打ち上げられました。そして、この記録はそれまでクウェートが持っていた7万7,282発のギネス記録を最初の1分間で超えてしまったそうです。（ちなみに、打ち上げ数日本一の花火大会は長野県の「諏訪湖祭湖上花火大会」で、4万発です。）

Unit 13 April Fools' Day in Japan

海外と比較すると日本のエープリル・フールは控えめだとよくいわれます。あなたはもっと派手に 4 月 1 日を楽しみたいと思いますか。

Pre-Reading Vocabulary Task

次の語句の日本語の意味として最も適切なものを、A～H から選んで（　）に記入しましょう。

1. guess ~ 　　（　）　　A. ~を考え出す

2. think up ~ 　（　）　　B. 被害者、犠牲者

3. cruel 　　　（　）　　C. ~を言い当てる、~を推測する

4. victim 　　　（　）　　D. 年配の

5. suspect 　　（　）　　E. 残酷な

6. employee 　（　）　　F. 社員、従業員

7. confuse ~ 　（　）　　G. 容疑者

8. elderly 　　（　）　　H. ~を混乱させる

日本人はエープリル・フールを もっと楽しむべきだ

 CD 38

For

⬜1 April Fools' Day falls on April 1st every year. It is a day for playing pranks on friends, family or coworkers and also a day for spreading hoaxes.

⬜2 In Japan, very few people do anything on April Fools' Day. Perhaps it is time to change this for the following reasons.

⬜3 Firstly, we Japanese are too serious. We are always working hard, studying hard or rushing around to meet a deadline. Daily life can make us glum! Enjoying April Fools' Day might help to cheer us up.

⬜4 Secondly, in some countries it is common for newspapers or TV to put out fake stories on April Fools' Day. It is fun to read or watch the news on April Fools' Day and try to guess which story might be a hoax.

⬜5 Finally, thinking up a prank is interesting. It has to be funny but not too cruel. If it goes well, it can be hilarious and, of course, the victim might aim to get revenge the following year! That is fun, too.

 CD 39

Against

⬜6 April Fools' Day may be popular in other countries but, for several reasons, there is no need for Japan to adopt this custom.

⬜7 First, it seems that playing a prank on someone is cruel. A friend of mine in the United States was pranked by his friends on April Fools' Day. They sent him a letter saying that he was a suspect in a crime and must go to the police station. He actually went! However, the police officer was laughing… the date on the letter was April 1st.

⬜8 Second, if a prank is played at work, then it is wasting company time. Employees are very busy and need to complete their tasks smoothly and efficiently. Pranks at work will cause problems and decrease worker productivity.

⬜9 Lastly, hoax news stories in newspapers or on TV can confuse people, particularly elderly people. Although most people can spot the fake stories, some people are gullible. The hoax news might make people anxious.

Note

fall on ~ ~に当たる　**play pranks on ~** ~にいたずらをする（prank は「いたずら、悪ふざけ」の意味）　**coworker** 同僚　**hoax** 作り話、でっち上げ　**rush around** 走り回る　**meet a deadline** 締め切りに間に合わせる（meet は「（要求などを）満たす」の意味）　**glum** 陰気な　**put out ~** ~を流す、発表する　**fake story** 偽の記事　**hilarious** 笑いを誘う　**aim to do** …しようと計画する　**get revenge** 復讐する　**company time** 勤務時間　**smoothly** 円滑に　**worker productivity** 労働者の生産性　**spot ~** ~を見抜く　**gullible** だまされやすい

Comprehension

次の文は本文の内容を要約したものです。該当する段落の番号を空欄に書き入れて、for または against のどちらに書かれているか○で囲んでください。

❶ People might be worried by hoax news stories. [ ] for　against

❷ It is unkind to play a prank on someone. [ ] for　against

❸ April Fools' Day can lift our spirits. [ ] for　against

❹ Fake news stories are interesting. [ ] for　against

❺ It is fun to plan a prank and the result may be entertaining. [ ] for　against

❻ Pranks are not suitable in the workplace. [ ] for　against

Grammar Point 目的語が動名詞と不定詞で意味の異なる他動詞

1. try

　*It is fun to … **try to** guess which story might be a hoax.* ［第4段落］

　*try to do は「~しようと試みる」、try ~ing は「（試しに）~してみる」の意味。

　例）He tried moving the sofa, and found it was very heavy.

2. need

　*Employees … **need to** complete their tasks smoothly and efficiently.* ［第8段落］

　*need to do は「~する必要がある」、need ~ing は「~される必要がある」の意味。

　例）This computer needs repairing.

　　　= This computer needs to be repaired.

Writing

以下の例文を参考にしながら、「**人を〜にする、人に〜させる**」という表現を学習しましょう。まずは、本文中の Against のセクションから次の文を探してください。

1. The hoax news might **make** people anxious.

ある行為や物事の結果について述べるときに **<make＋人＋形容詞/動詞：人を〜にする/人に〜させる>** の表現は役に立ちます。For のセクションにも同様の文があるので探してみましょう。

別の例文も紹介します。参考にしてください。

2. In the worst case, a prank might **make** people angry or even violent.
3. I was pranked last April Fools' Day, but it **made** me smile.

それでは賛成か反対の立場を決めた上で、学習した表現を使用しながら、英語で空欄を埋めてみましょう。

FOR : We should enjoy April Fools' Day more. ＿＿＿＿＿＿＿＿＿＿＿

＿＿＿＿＿＿＿＿＿＿＿＿＿＿＿＿＿＿＿＿＿＿＿＿＿＿＿＿＿＿

OR

AGAINST : We do not need April Fools' Day. ＿＿＿＿＿＿＿＿＿＿

＿＿＿＿＿＿＿＿＿＿＿＿＿＿＿＿＿＿＿＿＿＿＿＿＿＿＿＿＿＿

Listening Dictation

音声を聞いて次の空欄を埋めましょう。

1. The [1] (　　　　　) of April Fools' Day is not good for students in Japan because they are [2] (　　　　) with the new school year.

2. One of the most [1] (　　　　　) April Fools' hoax news stories was about [2] (　　　　　) growing on trees. Many people believed it!

3. In the past, many people sent prank letters on April Fools' Day. However, these days, if we send a prank email, the [1] (　　　　) may think it is junk mail and [2] (　　　　) it.

Speaking

次の会話モデルを使用して、クラスメートや先生にあなたの意見を伝えてみましょう。また、先ほど学習した表現も積極的に使いましょう。

A：Do you think we should enjoy April Fools' Day more in Japan?

B：Interesting question!

　　Well, yes, I do.

　　or

　　Actually, no, I don't.

A：What are your reasons?

B：[reason]＿＿＿＿＿＿＿＿＿＿＿＿＿＿＿＿＿＿＿＿

A：Sure. Anything else?

B：Also, [reason]＿＿＿＿＿＿＿＿＿＿＿＿＿＿＿＿＿

A：I see.

B：How about you? What do you think?

A：I (also) think we should.

　　or

　　I (also) think we don't have to celebrate April Fools' Day.

B：Why's that?

A：[reason]＿＿＿＿＿＿＿＿＿＿＿＿＿＿＿＿＿＿＿＿

B：OK. By the way, can you think of a good prank for April Fools' Day?

A：Ha ha. [idea]＿＿＿＿＿＿＿＿＿＿＿＿＿＿＿＿＿

　　本文中にも書かれていますが、海外メディアが4月1日にうそのニュースを流すことは珍しいことではありません。
　　例えば、日本の NHK に当たる BBC（英国放送協会）は空飛ぶペンギンの映像を2008年4月1日に放送しました。エープリル・フールに慣れているはずの英国の人たちも、そのリアルな映像にだまされて、テレビ局に問い合わせが殺到したそうです。興味があれば "BBC / flying penguin" で Google 検索すると、実際の映像を見ることができます。ぜひチェックしてみてください。一見の価値があります。

Unit 14 Summer-Vacation Assignments

夏休みといえば真っ先に宿題を思い浮かべる人も少なくないかもしれません。
あなたは、夏休みの宿題についてどのような考えを持っていますか。

Pre-Reading Vocabulary Task

次の語の日本語の意味として最も適切なものを、A～Hから選んで（　　）に記入しましょう。

1. commonly	（　）	**A.**	利点
2. burden	（　）	**B.**	一般に、普通に
3. complete ～	（　）	**C.**	負担
4. benefit	（　）	**D.**	～を観察する
5. observe ～	（　）	**E.**	賢く
6. survey	（　）	**F.**	～を終わらせる
7. wisely	（　）	**G.**	定期的に
8. regularly	（　）	**H.**	調査

夏休みの宿題はなくすべきだ

 41

For

① Starting at elementary school, continuing through junior and senior high school and even at college, summer-vacation assignments are commonly given to students in Japan.

② Despite their popularity with educators, we propose that summer-vacation assignments should be abolished for the following three reasons.   5

③ Firstly, almost all students consider vacation assignments to be a tiresome burden and therefore put the minimum effort into completing the work. As a result, the assignments become almost meaningless.

④ Secondly, not everything is learned through school work. Young   10 people must learn about life, too. Trying new things and gaining new experiences in the long summer vacation help young people to develop as humans.

⑤ Finally, especially in the case of young children, parents often have to help a lot with assignments. The assignments become a   15 burden for parents, too, and can even create bad feelings between the parent and child.

 42

Against

⑥ Summer-vacation assignments for students are common in Japan and overseas. Many people, both young and old, recognize the benefits of this study.   20

⑦ First, summer-vacation assignments are actually very interesting. In the case of an independent research project, students can choose the topic themselves. Students might choose to observe wildlife or to interview people for a survey. Such activities are surely more interesting than standard textbook-based homework.   25

⑧ Second, these assignments require independent thought and initiative. As such, they are much more like tasks in the real world. Therefore, vacation assignments help students to gain skills they need in their future careers.

⑨ Finally, doing assignments in the vacation helps students to learn   30 how to use their time wisely. For example, it is much better to do a little bit of the assignment regularly than to do it all on the last day of the summer holiday.

elementary school 小学校　assignment 宿題(= homework)　educator 教師　tiresome 面倒な　put the minimum effort into doing …するのに最低限の努力しかしない　meaningless 無意味な　not everything ~ すべてのことが~というわけではない〔部分否定〕　school work 学業　in the case of ~ ~の場合　a lot たくさん〔副詞的〕　bad feelings わだかまり　independent research project 自由研究課題　themselves 自ら、彼ら自身で　wildlife 野生動物　textbook-based 教科書に基づいた　independent thought 独自の思考　initiative 自発性　as such だから　be much more like ~ ~にはるかに近い　career 職業

Comprehension

次の文は本文の内容を要約したものです。該当する段落の番号を空欄に書き入れて、for または against のどちらに書かれているか○で囲んでください。

❶ Vacation assignments can teach skills that are useful for jobs.　☐　for　against

❷ Students do not put a lot of energy into completing vacation assignments.　☐　for　against

❸ Students can learn time-management skills.　☐　for　against

❹ Assignments can have a negative impact on family relationships.　☐　for　against

❺ Students can choose an interesting topic for their assignment.　☐　for　against

❻ Rather than more school work, students should use the vacation to learn about life.　☐　for　against

Grammar Point 　can の用法

1. 能力・可能:「~できる」

*In the case of an independent research project, students **can** choose the topic themselves.*［第7段落］

　＊上の文の can は「可能」を表している。

　例) The students can speak English very well.（能力）

2. 可能性:「~であり得る、~することがある」

*The assignments … **can** even create bad feelings between the parent and child.*［第5段落］

　＊否定文で使われると「~であるはずがない」という意味になる。

　例) You can't be hungry. You've just had breakfast.

Writing

以下の例文を参考にしながら、「(人が) ～するのに役立つ」という表現を学習しましょう。まずは、本文中の For のセクションから次の文を探してください。

1. Trying new things and gaining new experiences in the long summer vacation **help** young people **to develop** as humans.

<help ＋ 人 ＋ to do>は、ある行動のメリットを強調する際に有効な表現です。Against のセクションにも同様の文が２つ使われています。確認しましょう。

例文をあと２つ紹介します。参考にしてください。

2. Summer-vacation assignments **help** students **to learn** new things by themselves.
3. Taking a trip in the summer vacation **helps** young people **to broaden** their horizons.

それでは賛成か反対の立場を決めた上で、学習した表現を使用しながら、英語で空欄を埋めてみましょう。

FOR : I disagree with summer-vacation assignments. Instead, students should _____ in the summer vacation. Doing this helps students to

_____

OR

AGAINST : I think summer-vacation assignments are good. They help students to _____

Listening Dictation

 43

音声を聞いて次の空欄を埋めましょう。

1. For one of my elementary school summer assignments, I measured the
   1) (   ) of various 2) (   ) found around the home.

2. Planning assignments and marking finished assignments must be
   1) (   ), so summer-vacation homework might also be a
   2) (   ) on teachers, too.

3. My favorite proverb is "All 1) (   ) and no 2) (   ) makes Jack a dull boy." Thus I believe that kids should play a lot during the holidays.

Speaking

次の会話モデルを使用して、クラス
メートや先生にあなたの意見を伝え
てみましょう。また、先ほど学習した
表現も積極的に使いましょう。

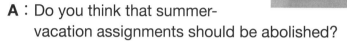

A：Do you think that summer-
vacation assignments should be abolished?

B：Tough question! Well... I suppose...

　　yes, I do.

　　or

　　no, I don't.

A：Really? How come?

B：First, [reason]＿＿＿＿＿＿＿＿＿＿＿＿＿＿＿＿＿＿＿＿＿＿＿＿

A：Sure. Any other reasons?

B：Also, [reason]＿＿＿＿＿＿＿＿＿＿＿＿＿＿＿＿＿＿＿＿＿＿＿＿＿

A：I see.

B：How about you? What do you think?

A：Actually, I think they should be abolished (too).

　　or

　　Actually, I think we should keep them (too).

B：Why's that?

A：[reason]＿＿＿＿＿＿＿＿＿＿＿＿＿＿＿＿＿＿＿＿＿＿＿＿＿＿＿＿

　　　小中学生の子どもを持つ保護者を対象に、子どもたちの夏休みの宿
題の進め方に関する調査が実施されました。結果は以下の通りです。
　・気が向いたときにやっていた … 39%
　・計画を立てて、その通りにやっていた … 34%
　・夏休みの終わりにまとめてやっていた … 16%
　・夏休み中に終わらなかった … 4%
　・そもそも宿題がなかった … 0.3%
　・その他 … 6.7%
　あなたはどのタイプでしたか。

Unit 15 Halloween Is Best!

好きな順に番号を書き入れてクラスメートと比べてみましょう

ハロウィーンはここ最近大きな盛り上がりを見せていますが、定番となっている外国のお祭りの中であなたが一番好きなものは何ですか。

Pre-Reading Vocabulary Task

次の語の日本語の意味として最も適切なものを、A～Hから選んで（　　）に記入しましょう。

1. major	（　）	**A.**	怖い、恐ろしい	
2. favorite	（　）	**B.**	信じられないほどに	
3. objectively	（　）	**C.**	お気に入り（の）	
4. decoration	（　）	**D.**	幽霊	
5. ghost	（　）	**E.**	装飾	
6. scary	（　）	**F.**	客観的に	
7. incredibly	（　）	**G.**	正直な	
8. honest	（　）	**H.**	主要な	

日本で一番楽しい外国のお祭りは
ハロウィーンだ

 44

For

[1] All of the major foreign festivals are celebrated in Japan.

[2] Perhaps you have a favorite among them but, objectively speaking, Halloween is the best one for Japanese people to enjoy for the following reasons.

5

[3] First, Japan has a dressing-up culture called cosplay. Halloween is the perfect festival for cosplaying and gives young people in Japan a wonderful opportunity to dress up. In fact, Japanese Halloween parades are now world-famous.

[4] In addition, Halloween has the cutest decorations. Ornamental Jack-

10 o'-lanterns, ghosts or even Jack Skellington and Sally figurines are fun to put up and look both charming and mysterious.

[5] Finally, Japan has a deep culture of scary stories and movies. Halloween is the perfect season to celebrate this culture by inviting friends round to watch a DVD of *The Ring* or *The Grudge*... while hiding

15 behind a cushion, of course.

 45

Against

[6] Halloween is definitely a fun festival but it is not necessarily the best foreign festival celebrated in Japan. Please think about the following points.

[7] Christmas is better than the rest for the following reasons: the

20 Christmas food in Japan is unique and delicious, Christmas falls during the school holidays and, above all, the Christmas lights in Japan are incredibly beautiful.

[8] On the other hand, although Halloween and Christmas are good, surely Valentine's Day is the best foreign festival. If you have a sweet tooth

25 and a romantic heart, Valentine's Day in Japan will bring joy and excitement.

[9] But, let's be honest. Halloween, Christmas and Valentine's Day get a little monotonous every year. The best foreign festivals are the minor ones that we do not know so well. Festivals such as St. Patrick's

30 Day or Mardi Gras are fresh and interesting.

Note

Halloween ハロウィーン　**dressing-up culture** 仮装の文化（dress up は「仮装する」の意味）
cosplay コスプレ（「コスチューム・プレイ」を語源とする和製英語だが、今では英国の辞書にも載っ
ている）　**ornamental** 装飾用の　**Jack-o'-lantern** カボチャちょうちん（カボチャをくり抜い
て中にロウソクをともす）　**Jack Skellington and Sally figurines** ジャック・スケリントンと
サリー（映画『ナイトメアー・ビフォア・クリスマス』の主人公とヒロイン）のフィギュア　**put
up** 飾り付けをする　***The Ring***（日本のホラー映画『リング』）　***The Grudge***（日本のホラー映画
『呪怨（じゅおん）』のハリウッドリメイク版）　**Christmas lights** クリスマスのイルミネーション
have a sweet tooth 甘い物が好きだ　**monotonous** 退屈な　**St. Patrick's Day** セントパト
リック・デー（アイルランドにキリスト教を広めた聖人パトリックの功績をたたえる祭り）　**Mardi
Gras** マルディ・グラ（米ルイジアナ州ニューオーリンズの世界的に有名なカーニバル）

Comprehension

次の文は本文の内容を要約したものです。該当する段落の番号を空欄に書き入れて、
for または against のどちらに書かれているか○で囲んでください。

❶ Not-so-famous foreign festivals are best. ☐　for　against

❷ In fact, Christmas is the best festival. ☐　for　against

❸ Japan has a great culture of dressing up. ☐　for　against

❹ It is a great festival for watching movies. ☐　for　against

❺ In fact, Valentine's Day is the best festival. ☐　for　against

❻ It is the festival with the best decorations. ☐　for　against

Grammar Point 　部分否定と全否定

1. 部分否定：「すべてが〜とは限らない」

   *... but it is **not necessarily** the best foreign festival celebrated in Japan.*
   ［第6段落］

   ＊否定語とともに all, always, every などのような語が用いられると部分否定に
   なる。上の文は「必ずしも〜とは限らない」の意味。

2. 全否定：「（まったく）〜ない」

   例）Halloween is not [never] the best foreign festival celebrated in Japan.

Writing

以下の例文を参考にしながら、「…に最適な～だ」という表現を学習しましょう。
まずは、本文中の For のセクションから次の文を探してください。

   1. Halloween **is the perfect** festival **for** cosplaying...

<A is the perfect ～ for... > や < A is the perfect～to do> という表現
は、あるものが特定の目的に最も適していることを伝える手段としてよく使用され
ます。For のセクションにもう１つ同様の文があります。確認しましょう。

他にも例文を挙げておきます。

   2. New Year's Eve **is the perfect** evening **for** a party.
   3. Putting on a vampire costume **is the perfect** way **to** dress up at
      Halloween.

それでは賛成か反対の立場を決めた上で、学習した表現を使用しながら、英語で空
欄を埋めてみましょう。

FOR : Halloween is the best foreign festival. It is the perfect _____

for/to _____

OR

AGAINST : In fact, _____ is the best foreign festival. It is the perfect

_____ for/to _____

Listening Dictation

音声を聞いて次の空欄を埋めましょう。

1. Halloween is the perfect time for making unique [1] (   ), especially
   using [2] (   ) as an ingredient.

2. Some foreign festivals such as [1] (   ) Day are [2] (   )
   celebrated at all in Japan.

3. Easter [1] (   ) are delicious and Easter motifs such as chicks and
   [2] (   ) are cute, yet Easter is still a minor foreign festival in Japan.

Speaking

次の会話モデルを使用して、クラス
メートや先生にあなたの意見を伝え
てみましょう。また、先ほど学習した
表現も積極的に使いましょう。

A：Which do you think is the
　　 best foreign festival celebrated in Japan?

B：For me, ＿＿＿＿＿＿＿＿＿＿＿＿ is the best.

A：Interesting! Why's that?

B：Well, [reason]＿＿＿＿＿＿＿＿＿＿＿＿＿＿＿＿＿＿＿

A：OK. Any other reasons?

B：Also, [reason]＿＿＿＿＿＿＿＿＿＿＿＿＿＿＿＿＿＿＿＿

A：I see.

B：How about you? Which do you think is the best?

A：I (also) think ＿＿＿＿＿＿＿＿＿＿＿＿ is best.

B：Why's that?

A：[reason]＿＿＿＿＿＿＿＿＿＿＿＿＿＿＿＿＿＿＿＿＿＿＿＿＿

B：I see. How did you celebrate it last time?

A：＿＿＿＿＿＿＿＿＿＿＿＿＿＿＿＿＿＿＿＿＿＿＿＿＿＿＿＿

　　日本では仮装の日となりつつあるハロウィーンですが、そもそも仮
装をする理由をご存知でしょうか。
　　ハロウィーンは古代ケルト人が行っていた宗教行事が起源だといわ
れています。彼らの暦では1年の始まりが11月1日と定められてい
て、その前日の10月31日の夜に、先祖の霊が家族を訪ねて来ると信
じられていました。しかし、その霊に混じって悪霊や魔女が生きてい
る人の魂を奪いに来るとも考えられていたため、人々は自分が人間だ
と気付かれないように、自ら魔物や魔女の仮装をして自分の身を守り
ました。これがハロウィーンにおける仮装の始まりとされています。
（仮装は、悪霊を怖がらせて追い払うという魔除けの意味もあったよ
うです。）

Unit 16 Valentine's Day in Japan

欧米ではバレンタインデーに男性が女性に花を贈るのが一般的なようです。女性が男性にチョコレートを贈る日本のバレンタインデーをあなたはどう思いますか。

Pre-Reading Vocabulary Task

次の語句の日本語の意味として最も適切なものを、A〜Hから選んで（　　）に記入しましょう。

1. (be) celebrated	（　）	A. やめられる、捨てられる
2. male	（　）	B. 〜を無視する
3. (be) abandoned	（　）	C. 祝われる
4. artificial	（　）	D. さらに
5. ignore 〜	（　）	E. 男性（の）
6. adopt 〜	（　）	F. 〜を取り入れる
7. above all	（　）	G. 人為的な、人工の
8. in addition	（　）	H. 何はさておき、とりわけ

日本のバレンタインデーは変えるべきだ

 CD 47

For

[1] Valentine's Day adds color and fun to the cold days of February. It is certainly an enjoyable festival day, but recently people have been questioning the way it is celebrated in Japan.

[2] In fact, we should change our style of Valentine's Day for the following reasons.

[3] The first point is that the pressure on women at work to give chocolate to male coworkers is not good. It could even be seen as a kind of workplace harassment. This custom should definitely be abandoned.

[4] Secondly, even if men receive chocolate on Valentine's Day, many do not give a gift in return. There is an artificial festival day in March called White Day for men to give a gift, but many men forget or even ignore White Day.

[5] Finally, we could adopt customs from abroad for Valentine's Day. For example, in England both men and women use Valentine's Day to send an anonymous card to someone that they secretly love. It sounds fun.

 CD 48

 Against

[6] Japanese-style Valentine's Day might be different from Valentine's Day in other countries but it definitely has some good points.

[7] There is no need to change Valentine's Day in Japan for the following reasons.

[8] Above all, Japanese-style Valentine's Day is unique. Many foreign people are interested to hear about it from their Japanese friends. In fact, other countries in Asia have started to adopt the Japanese style.

[9] In addition, we can also consider the economy. There is a huge rush to buy chocolate before and on Valentine's Day in Japan. This is good for both confectionery companies and for retailers.

[10] Last but not least, Valentine's Day in Japan is simple. Women need not worry about what kind of present to buy... chocolate is OK every year!

Note

color 彩り　**the way it is celebrated in Japan**（the way (that / in which) ... の形で「…の仕方、…する方法」を表す）　**coworker** 同僚　**a kind of ～** 一種の～　**workplace harassment** 職場での嫌がらせ　**in return** お返しに　**anonymous** 匿名の　**There is a huge rush to do** …するために多くの人が殺到する　**confectionery company** 製菓会社　**retailer** 小売業者　**last but not least** 大事なことを言い忘れたが

Comprehension

次の文は本文の内容を要約したものです。該当する段落の番号を空欄に書き入れて、for または against のどちらに書かれているか○で囲んでください。

① It could be a chance to adopt customs from other countries.　☐　for　against

② A gift in return is not always given.　☐　for　against

③ It is unique.　☐　for　against

④ Women may feel unwanted pressure to buy chocolate.　☐　for　against

⑤ It gives a boost to the economy.　☐　for　against

⑥ This style is easy and simple.　☐　for　against

Grammar Point 　不定詞の意味上の主語：for ～ to do

*There is an artificial festival day in March called White Day **for** men **to** give a gift ...*［第4段落］

＊上の文では men が give a gift の意味上の主語を示す。そしてこの to 不定詞は形容詞用法なので、「～が…するための」と訳すことができる。

例１）It is a mistake for the government to cancel the plan.（名詞用法）

例２）He held the door open for her to enter the classroom.（副詞用法）

78

Writing

以下の例文を参考にしながら、「〜にとって…だ」という表現を学習しましょう。
まずは、本文中の Against のセクションから次の文を探してください。

1. This **is good for** both confectionery companies and for retailers.

<X is good for Y.> は実にシンプルな表現ですが、さまざまな形容詞を使うことでいろいろな言い方ができます。肯定的なものでも否定的なものでも議論の場などで役に立つ表現です。

他の例文も紹介しておきます。

2. Japanese-style Valentine's Day **is great for** people who like making sweets.

3. Eating a lot of chocolate **is bad for** people's health.

4. Valentine's Day **can be tough for** guys who never get any chocolate.

それでは賛成か反対の立場を決めた上で、学習した表現を使用しながら、英語で空欄を埋めてみましょう。

FOR : I think Japanese-style Valentine's Day should be changed. _____

_____

OR

AGAINST : I think Japanese-style Valentine's Day should be kept as it

is. _____

Listening Dictation

 49

音声を聞いて次の空欄を埋めましょう。

1. If the custom was for men and women to [1] (　　　　　) chocolate on Valentine's Day, White Day would be [2] (　　　　　).

2. Recently, Japanese women have been using Valentine's Day as an [1] (　　　　) to buy [2] (　　　　　) chocolate.

3. In many countries, men and women give each other a wide [1] (　　　　　) of gifts on Valentine's Day, [2] (　　　　) [3] (　　　　) flowers, clothing and jewelry.

Speaking

次の会話モデルを使用して、クラス
メートや先生にあなたの意見を伝え
てみましょう。また、先ほど学習した
表現も積極的に使いましょう。

A：What do you think about
　　Japanese-style Valentine's Day?

B：I think it should be changed.

　　or

　　I think it is OK as it is.

A：I see. Why's that?

B：[reason]_____

A：Is that so? Any other reasons?

B：Also, [reason]_____

A：Thanks for sharing your opinions.

B：How about you? What do you think?

A：As for me, I (also) think it should be changed.

　　or

　　As for me, I (also) think it should stay the same.

B：Can you give me a reason?

A：Sure. [reason]_____

　　本文中で英国のカードについて触れられていたのでもう少し補足し
ます。バレンタインデーに好きな人に匿名のカードを送る風習は19
世紀から始まったといわれています。シャイな英国人ならではの習慣
ですが、カードに差出人の名前を書くと不吉なことが起こると考えら
れていたという説もあります。

　　受け取った人はたいていの場合、筆跡やイニシャルなどのヒントか
ら相手が分かるようですが、中には何年間も差出人が分からないまま
という実に悲しいケースも存在するそうです。

Unit 17 Smartphone Lock Screens

私は暗証番号派

僕は指紋認証派

僕はこれを使っています

スマートフォンのロックを解除するにはいろいろな方法があります。あなたは生体認証とパスワード（暗証番号）入力、どちらを使っていますか。

Pre-Reading Vocabulary Task

次の語句の日本語の意味として最も適切なものを、A～Hから選んで（　）に記入しましょう。

1. more and more （　　） **A.** 適切な

2. offer ～ 　　（　　） **B.** ～を提供する

3. appropriate 　（　　） **C.** ～を手に入れる

4. undoubtedly 　（　　） **D.** 間違いなく

5. gain ～ 　　　（　　） **E.** ～を拒否する

6. available 　　（　　） **F.** ますます

7. secure 　　　（　　） **G.** 利用できる

8. refuse ～ 　　（　　） **H.** 安全な

スマホのロック解除には
パスワードよりも生体認証だ

 50

For

[1] Biometric lock screens such as fingerprint-sensor lock screens and facial-recognition lock screens have become more and more popular on smartphones recently.

[2] These are the best lock screens for the following reasons.

[3] Firstly, these technologies offer a very high level of security. Nobody has the same fingerprint as you and nobody has the same face as you. This means that it is almost impossible for somebody to access your phone.

[4] Secondly, these technologies are very convenient. In order to access your phone, all you need to do is press your finger on it or just look at it. In this world where convenience is highly valued, biometric lock screens are the most appropriate type.

[5] Finally, technology should be cool and enjoyable. Biometric lock screens are undoubtedly very cool and by using them we can gain greater enjoyment from our smartphones.

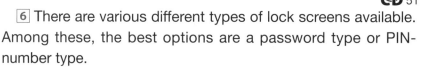 51

Against

[6] There are various different types of lock screens available. Among these, the best options are a password type or PIN-number type.

[7] Firstly, these are very secure options. For many years, people have used passwords for email accounts and PIN numbers for ATM cards and therefore these are methods that we know and trust.

[8] Secondly, it is possible to change passwords and PIN numbers. This means that we can choose a new code if necessary. Biometric access methods work by measuring parts of your body, and these of course cannot be changed.

[9] Thirdly, there is never a problem with access via a password or PIN number. As long as you type in the correct code, you can always access your phone. On the other hand, biometric methods sometimes refuse access, even for the person authorized to use the phone.

Note

biometric 生体認証による **lock screen** ロック画面 **fingerprint-sensor** 指紋センサーによる **facial-recognition** 顔認識による **the same A as B** Bと同じA **all you need to do is do** …するだけでいい **cool** かっこいい〔口語〕 **PIN-number** 暗証番号の（PIN は personal identification number の略語） **access method** アクセス方法 **via ~** ~による **as long as ~** ~する限りは **type in ~** ~を入力する **(be) authorized to do** …する権限が与えられている

Comprehension

次の文は本文の内容を要約したものです。該当する段落の番号を空欄に書き入れて、for または against のどちらに書かれているか○で囲んでください。

❶ Password and PIN-number lock screens offer good security.　☐　for　against

❷ Fingerprint-sensor and facial-recognition lock screens are secure.　☐　for　against

❸ These lock screens are easy to change if necessary.　☐　for　against

❹ These lock screens are fun to use.　☐　for　against

❺ The system will not give false errors with these lock screens.　☐　for　against

❻ Convenience is an advantage of these lock screens.　☐　for　against

Grammar Point 　関係・関連を表す with

*Thirdly, there is never a problem **with** access via a password or PIN number.*
［第9段落］

* with には「同伴（~と一緒に）」や「手段（~を用いて）」、「所有（~を持っている）」などさまざまな意味があるが、ここでは「関係・関連（~に関しては、~については）」を表している。

例1）Do you have a problem with that?

例2）What's the matter with you?

Writing

以下の例文を参考にしながら、「**これは…を意味する**」という表現を学習しましょう。
まずは、本文中の For のセクションから次の文を探してください。

1. Nobody has the same fingerprint as you and nobody has the same face as you. **This means that** it is almost impossible for somebody to access your phone.

ある物事の結果や影響を分かりやすく説明したいときに、**<This means that ... >** の形を使うことができます。Against のセクションにも同様の文があるので探してみましょう。

例文をあと2つ挙げておきます。

2. Technology is improving. **This means that** there are more options for lock screens.
3. I often wear a mask. **This means that** a facial-recognition lock screen might not be the best choice for me.

それでは賛成か反対の立場を決めた上で、学習した表現を使用しながら、英語で空欄を埋めてみましょう。

FOR : _____

      This means that _____

OR

AGAINST : _____

      This means that _____

Listening Dictation   52

音声を聞いて次の空欄を埋めましょう。

1. I guess that each type of lock screen has ^1)(   ) and ^2)(   ).

2. I have been using my fingerprint to ^1)(   ) my phone and it has been very ^2)(   ) so far.

3. On a crowded train, I sometimes worry that a stranger is ^1)(   ) over my ^2)(   ) when I enter my smartphone password.

Speaking

次の会話モデルを使用して、クラスメートや先生にあなたの意見を伝えてみましょう。また、先ほど学習した表現も積極的に使いましょう。

A：What type of lock screen do you use to access your smartphone?

B：I use (a password / a fingerprint sensor / facial recognition).

A：Really? How come?

B：Well, [reason]_____

A：Sure. Any other reasons?

B：Also, [reason]_____

A：I see.

B：How about you? How do you access your smartphone?

A：I use_____

　　　or

　　　I also use_____

B：Why's that?

A：[reason]_____

COLUMN

　スマートフォンに入っている大切な情報を守るためにロックを掛けている人は少なくないでしょう。現在では指紋認証をはじめとする生体認証が一般的ですが、「ピースサインをして撮った写真からその人の指紋データが再現できる」というニュースが話題となったように、生体認証だから必ずしも安全というわけではありません。

　最近では、個人認証に心拍数や体臭、さらには起床時間やアプリの利用履歴などの行動パターンを活用したシステムも開発されているようですが、100％安全な認証方法が導入される日は果たして来るのでしょうか。

Unit 18 YouTube vs. Normal TV

YouTube をはじめとする動画共有サービスの流行で、テレビを見ない人が増えているようです。あなたはテレビと YouTube どちらをよく見ますか。

Pre-Reading Vocabulary Task

次の語句の日本語の意味として最も適切なものを、A〜H から選んで（　　）に記入しましょう。

1. according to 〜	（　）	A. 信頼できない
2. previous	（　）	B. 快適な
3. amount	（　）	C. 量
4. several	（　）	D. 情報源、出所
5. comfortable	（　）	E. 以前の
6. in terms of 〜	（　）	F. いくつかの
7. unreliable	（　）	G. 〜に応じて、〜によれば
8. source	（　）	H. 〜に関して、〜の点から

見るならテレビよりも
YouTube だ

 53

For

[1] In the past, television was the main option for evening entertainment. These days, however, people have more choice. Many young people enjoy watching YouTube and, in fact, this is a better choice than watching TV.

[2] First, we can watch content on YouTube according to our own schedule. There is no need to sit in front of the screen at a certain time or record programs to watch later. With YouTube, when we are ready to watch, we can watch.

[3] Second, YouTube has a lot of fresh and interesting content. There are unique YouTubers doing interesting things and their content is updated regularly. Television seems to have become stale. For example, each new TV drama seems very similar to previous dramas.

[4] Finally, the amount of advertising on YouTube is much less than on TV. Sometimes when watching TV, it almost seems as though half of the program time consists of commercials. YouTube commercials are short and can even be skipped before they are finished.

 54

Against

[5] YouTube may be popular these days, but the truth is that watching TV is a better option. There are several reasons for this.

[6] First, Japanese television dramas are very interesting and feature young and attractive actors and actresses. Such dramas can only be enjoyed on TV. In addition, the so-called "wide shows" feature many entertaining celebrities.

[7] Second, generally speaking, it is more comfortable to watch TV. We can lie on the floor or sofa and completely relax while enjoying our favorite TV shows.

[8] Finally, in terms of news and documentaries, content on the Internet may be unreliable. In the worst cases, some people have been fooled into believing "fake news." If we want reliable factual information, the TV is a much better source.

Comprehension

次の文は本文の内容を要約したものです。該当する段落の番号を空欄に書き入れて、for または against のどちらに書かれているか○で囲んでください。

1 It is nice to relax on a sofa or on the floor and watch a big screen.　　　　　[　]　for　against

2 YouTube content is new and fascinating.　　　　　[　]　for　against

3 We can watch YouTube clips whenever we like.　　　　　[　]　for　against

4 Advertising is less annoying on YouTube.　　　　　[　]　for　against

5 Information from the Internet may not be reliable.　　　　　[　]　for　against

6 TV dramas and other programs are very entertaining.　　　　　[　]　for　against

Grammar Point 　差が大きいことを表す much ＋ 比較級（＋than）

1. *Finally, the amount of advertising on YouTube is **much less than** on TV.*
   ［第4段落］

2. *If we want reliable factual information, the TV is a **much better** source.*
   ［第8段落］

   *比較される２者の差が大きいことを表す場合、比較級の前に「はるかに、ずっと」を意味する much や far などを置く。差が小さい時は**<a little [a bit] ＋ 比較級 ＋ (than)>**を用いる。

   例）The new machine is a little bigger than the previous model.

Writing

以下の例文を参考にしながら、「~する必要がない」という表現を学習しましょう。まずは、本文中の For のセクションから次の文を探してください。

1. First, we can watch content on YouTube according to our own schedule. **There is no need to** sit in front of the screen at a certain time...

このほかにも「~する必要がない」を意味する表現がいくつかあります。以下のパターンを見てみましょう。

2. I prefer _____ because **there is no need to**...

3. I prefer _____ because **it is not necessary to**...

4. I prefer _____ because **we do not have to**...

それでは賛成か反対の立場を決めた上で、学習した表現を使用しながら、その理由を英語で書いてみましょう。

FOR : I prefer watching YouTube because _____

_____

OR

AGAINST : I prefer watching TV because _____

_____

Listening Dictation

🎧 55

音声を聞いて次の空欄を埋めましょう。

1. To be ¹⁾ ( ), I enjoy ²⁾ ( ) watching YouTube clips and watching TV.

2. I actually ¹⁾ ( ) ²⁾ ( ) of my TV because I ³⁾ ( ) ⁴⁾ ( ) watch it.

3. ¹⁾ ( ) YouTube, I also watch Niconico quite ²⁾ ( ) because it has a lot of content ³⁾ ( ) to Japan.

Speaking

次の会話モデルを使用して、クラスメートや先生にあなたの意見を伝えてみましょう。また、先ほど学習した表現も積極的に使いましょう。

A：Which do you prefer in the evening, watching YouTube or watching TV?

B：That's a tricky question! I guess I prefer _____

A：That's interesting. Why?

B：Well, [reason]_____

A：I see. Anything else?

B：Also, [reason]_____

A：OK. Thanks for sharing.

B：How about you? Which do you prefer?

A：Actually, I like_____

　　　or

　　　I also like_____

B：Why's that?

A：[reason]_____

今回の議論そのものを台無しにしてしまうかもしれませんが、実は「テレビで YouTube の動画を見る方法」を検索すると、アプリや機器などに関するさまざまな情報を入手することができます。

また、インターネットに接続できて YouTube にも対応している次世代の「スマートテレビ」も各メーカーからすでに発売されていて、人々の注目を集めています。テレビで YouTube を見ることが当たり前になる時代はもうすぐそこかもしれません。

Unit 19 Internet vs. Bricks-and-Mortar

Shop

50% オフ
送料無料

お似合いですね

インターネットの普及により買い物がとても便利になりましたが、依然として不安な点も拭えません。あなたは実際の店舗とネットショップ、どちらで買い物をしたいですか。

Pre-Reading Vocabulary Task

次の語の日本語の意味として最も適切なものを、A〜Hから選んで（　　）に記入しましょう。

1. indicate 〜	（　）	**A.**	〜を購入する
2. purchase 〜	（　）	**B.**	〜を調べる
3. following	（　）	**C.**	〜を確認する
4. maintain 〜	（　）	**D.**	〜を過ごす、〜を費やす
5. genuine	（　）	**E.**	〜を指し示す
6. examine 〜	（　）	**F.**	本物の
7. confirm 〜	（　）	**G.**	〜を維持する
8. spend 〜	（　）	**H.**	次の

買い物するなら
お店よりもネットだ

 56

1 These days, the increasing number of net shoppers indicates that many people are satisfied with purchasing goods via the Internet. Indeed, it is better than bricks-and-mortar shopping for the following reasons.

5 **2** The first point, as you may have guessed, is convenience. Just switch on your PC and with just a few mouse clicks you can make an order. If you do not have a PC, no problem! You can use your smartphone.

3 Another great benefit of buying something on the Internet is price. 10 Because vendors do not have to maintain a physical store, items have very low prices and in many cases delivery is free.

4 The final point is connected to the previous point. We can easily compare the prices of different vendors on the Internet. That helps us to find the lowest price. Imagine trudging around several bricks-and-15 mortar shops to find the lowest price for an item... it would be exhausting!

 57

5 Internet shopping may be becoming more popular but, in fact, good old bricks-and-mortar shopping is better.

6 Please consider the following reasons.

20 **7** Firstly, think about fake products. When you purchase something from a web vendor, are you really getting a genuine product? Counterfeit goods can be a problem on the Internet, even from famous vendors.

8 The second point is connected to the first. When we buy goods at 25 a bricks-and-mortar store, we can easily examine and check the items carefully. We can look closely and confirm they are genuine. And of course for clothes, shoes and accessories, we can try them on to make sure that the fit is OK.

9 And lastly, do not forget that you can enjoy bricks-and-mortar 30 shopping with your friends. Simply put, it is a fun way to spend the day!

Note

net shopper オンラインショッピングの利用者　**via ~** ~を通じて　**bricks-and-mortar shopping** 実店舗でのショッピング（bricks-and-mortar は「れんがとモルタル（セメント）でできた」という意味で、オンライン店舗と対比した表現となっている）　**make an order** 注文する　**vendor** 販売業者　**physical store** 実店舗（physical には「実際の」という意味がある）　**trudge around ~** ~を歩き回る　**exhausting** とても疲れる　**counterfeit** 偽の（= fake）　**try ~ on** ~を身に着けてみる　**fit** フィット感、ぴったり加減　**simply put** 簡単に言えば（= to put it simply）

Comprehension

次の文は本文の内容を要約したものです。該当する段落の番号を空欄に書き入れて、for または against のどちらに書かれているか○で囲んでください。

1 It is more fun! ☐ for　against

2 Comparing prices is easy and so we can find the lowest price. ☐ for　against

3 Buying fake products is a possible problem. ☐ for　against

4 It is easy and simple to buy things. ☐ for　against

5 We can physically examine the products before buying. ☐ for　against

6 Prices are cheaper. ☐ for　against

Grammar Point do not have to と must not の違い

*Because vendors **do not have to** maintain a physical store, items have very low prices and in many cases delivery is free.* [第3段落]

＊have to「~しなければならない」の否定形である do not have to は「~しなくてもよい」という不必要の意味になる。「~してはいけない」という禁止を表す場合は must not を使用する。

例1）You don't have to talk so loud. I can hear you.

例2）You must not talk loudly in the library.

Writing

以下の例文を参考にしながら、「**簡単に〜できる、〜は容易だ**」という表現を学習しましょう。まずは、本文中の For のセクションから次の文を探してみましょう。

1. **We can easily** compare the prices of different vendors on the Internet.

簡単にできるからという理由を述べることが、自分の主張の裏付けになる場合があります。Against のセクションにも同様の表現が使用されているので確認しましょう。

次に、似たような意味を持つほかの表現も学習しましょう。

2. **It is easy to** purchase things on the Internet.
3. Try**ing** on clothes **is easy** at a bricks-and-mortar store.
4. **We can quickly** know if a product is real or fake at a bricks-and-mortar store.

それでは賛成か反対の立場を決めた上で、学習した表現を使用しながら、その理由を英語で書いてみましょう。

FOR : I think Internet shopping is better. _____

_____

OR

AGAINST : I think bricks-and-mortar shopping is better. _____

_____

Listening Dictation   58

音声を聞いて次の空欄を埋めましょう。

1. In my opinion, Internet shopping is good for buying [1] (　　　　　　　)
   but for [2] (　　　　　) I prefer buying things at a bricks-and-mortar store.

2. I heard that [1] (　　　　　) shopping on the Internet is becoming more
   and more popular these days, especially for busy [2] (　　　　) people.

3. Some people go to a bricks-and-mortar shop to [1] (　　　　) products,
   and then [2] (　　　　) buy the same product at a low price online!

94

Speaking

次の会話モデルを使用して、クラスメートや先生にあなたの意見を伝えてみましょう。また、先ほど学習した表現も積極的に使いましょう。

A：Which do you prefer, Internet shopping or bricks-and-mortar shopping?

B：Hmm... I think I prefer_____

A：OK. Why?

B：Well, [reason]_____

A：That's interesting. Any other reasons?

B：Also, [reason]_____

A：I see.

B：How about you? Which do you prefer?

A：I prefer_____

　　　or

　　　I also prefer_____

B：Why's that?

A：[reason]_____

B：I got it.

COLUMN

　　　毎日多くの人が利用しているネットショッピングですが、バーチャル・リアリティー（VR）の進化に伴い、その買い物体験がよりリアルなものに変わろうとしています。

　　　例えば、ネットショッピングで敬遠されがちな服や靴の購入時には、自分のサイズや撮影データを送信することで、等身大のアバターが商品を試着してくれるため、自分に合ったものを慎重に選ぶことができます。また、VRヘッドセットから香りを発生させる技術が開発されたことで、今後、焼きたてのパンなどの香りを自宅で体験しながら買い物ができるようになるそうです。

Translation Software

近年の翻訳ソフトの進化には目を見張るものあります。このソフトを英語の宿題に利用することについてあなたはどう思いますか。

Pre-Reading Vocabulary Task

次の語の日本語の意味として最も適切なものを、A〜Hから選んで（　　）に記入しましょう。

1. recently	（　）	**A.**	有名な
2. well-known	（　）	**B.**	学習者
3. amazingly	（　）	**C.**	特に
4. especially	（　）	**D.**	最近
5. sentence	（　）	**E.**	言い回し、表現
6. odd	（　）	**F.**	変な
7. learner	（　）	**G.**	驚くほど
8. expression	（　）	**H.**	文

英語の宿題に翻訳ソフトを使用しても構わない

 59

For

1 With smartphones and the Internet, students now have access to translation software whenever they want.

2 Students should be allowed to use translation software for their homework assignments for the following reasons.

3 First of all, in the future when they become members of society, 5 many students will need to use translation software at work. For example, company workers often use it to read and write emails in English. Given this reality, why not let students become proficient in using translation software as soon as possible?

4 Also, translation software has gotten much better recently. Well- 10 known services give amazingly good translations, especially for shorter sentences.

5 Finally, students can actually use translation software as an English-learning tool. If they read and study the English sentences produced by the software, it is certain that they can improve their 15 English skills.

 60

Against

6 It may be tempting for students to use translation software for English assignments but, for several reasons, this should not be allowed.

7 Let's think about why. 20

8 In the first place, there is no doubt that using translation software for an assignment is a kind of cheating. The sentences in the submitted work have been produced by a machine, not by the student.

9 In addition, when sentences are translated by machine, students do not know if they are correct or not. In many cases, the English that 25 is produced is odd and students do not recognize this. This is especially true for low-level learners.

10 Thirdly, unless students grapple with making their own original English sentences, their English level will not improve. Remember the famous expression, "You learn from your mistakes." If it is software 30 that is making the mistakes, you learn nothing.

Comprehension

次の文は本文の内容を要約したものです。該当する段落の番号を空欄に書き入れて、for または against のどちらに書かれているか○で囲んでください。

1 Translation software can be used to learn English.　　for　　against

2 Using translation software does not teach us anything.　　for　　against

3 Using translation software is cheating.　　for　　against

4 Translation services have improved.　　for　　against

5 Students may use translation software in their future workplace.　　for　　against

6 Students have no idea of the accuracy of the translated sentences.　　for　　against

Grammar Point 　　　強調構文：It is ～ that … 「…なのは～だ」

*If **it is** software **that** is making the mistakes, you learn nothing.* ［第10段落］

＊上の文は強調構文。なお、強調構文と形式主語構文の見分け方は以下のようになる。

It is と that 以外の語句を、語順を入れ替えるなどして文として成立すれば強調構文。

例1） It is in July that the festival is held.　⇒　The festival is held in July.
（強調構文）

例2） It is important that you study English every day.（形式主語構文）

Writing

以下の例文を参考にしながら、「**～は確かだ・疑いない**」という表現を学習しましょう。まずは、本文中の For のセクションから次の文を探してください。

1. If they read and study the English sentences produced by the software, **it is certain that** they can improve their English skills.

「**～は確かだ・疑いない**」という表現は議論の場でも使用されます。Against のセクションにも似たようなものがあるので確認しましょう。

ほかの例文も紹介しておきます。また 4 のように副詞を使用することもできます。

2. **It is certain that** using translation software saves time.
3. **There is no doubt that** students using translation software will be found out.
4. Using translation software **definitely** makes our lives easier.

それでは賛成か反対の立場を決めた上で、学習した表現を使用しながら、その理由を英語で書いてみましょう。

FOR : Students should be allowed to use translation software. _____

OR

AGAINST : Students should not be allowed to use translation software.

Listening Dictation

 61

音声を聞いて次の空欄を埋めましょう。

1. If it is near the 1) (   ) and I have no 2) (   ), then I might be tempted to use translation software for an English assignment.

2. It is becoming more and more 1) (   ) to 2) (   ) between work produced by humans and work produced by translation software.

3. It has been reported that some 1) (   ) are using specialist software to 2) (   ) English assignments.

Speaking

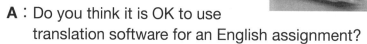

次の会話モデルを使用して、クラスメートや先生にあなたの意見を伝えてみましょう。また、先ほど学習した表現も積極的に使いましょう。

A：Do you think it is OK to use translation software for an English assignment?

B：Yes, I think it's acceptable.

　　or

　　No, I don't think it is acceptable.

A：I see. What are your reasons?

B：Well, [reason]＿＿＿＿＿＿＿＿＿＿＿＿＿＿＿＿＿

A：Anything else?

B：Also, [reason]＿＿＿＿＿＿＿＿＿＿＿＿＿＿＿＿＿

A：That's interesting.

B：How about you? What do you think?

A：I think it is acceptable/not acceptable, too.

　　or

　　Actually, I think it's acceptable/not acceptable.

B：Could you give a reason?

A：Sure. [reason]＿＿＿＿＿＿＿＿＿＿＿＿＿＿＿＿＿

翻訳ソフトのここ数年の急速な進化を見ると、近い将来、英語の授業で翻訳ソフトの活用法について教えるようになる可能性も否定できません。そこで一足早く、翻訳ソフトを使って英訳をする際に精度を上げるためのヒントを紹介します。
1. 主語・述語・目的語を入れるようにする
2. ややこしくないシンプルな日本語を入力する
3. なるべく漢字で入力する

念のために言っておきますが、翻訳ソフトを正しく使いこなすには相応の英語力が必要です。まずは自分の力で英訳や和訳をするように努力してください。

TEXT PRODUCTION STAFF

edited by	編集
Masato Kogame	小亀 正人
Kimio Sato	佐藤 公雄

English-language editing by	英文校閲
Bill Benfield	ビル・ベンフィールド

cover design by	表紙デザイン
Nobuyoshi Fujino	藤野 伸芳

illustrated by	イラスト
IOK Co., Ltd.	株式会社 イオック

CD PRODUCTION STAFF

recorded by	吹き込み者
Karen Haedrich (AmerE)	カレン・ヘドリック（アメリカ英語）
Dominic Allen (AmerE)	ドミニク・アレン（アメリカ英語）

Thanks to Tatsuya and Shiori.

Two Sides to Every Discussion 2
英語で考え、英語で発信する2

2020年1月20日　初版発行
2023年4月10日　第5刷発行

著　　者　Jonathan Lynch
　　　　　委文　光太郎

発 行 者　佐野 英一郎

発 行 所　株式会社 成 美 堂
　　　　　〒101-0052　東京都千代田区神田小川町3-22
　　　　　TEL 03-3291-2261　FAX 03-3293-5490
　　　　　https://www.seibido.co.jp

印刷・製本　三美印刷株式会社

ISBN 978-4-7919-7210-4　　　　　　　　　　Printed in Japan